W9-CRC-058

HOW TO INTERPRET
Dreams

ANNA FORNARI

CRESCENT BOOKS
New York

Dream interpretations A–Z and some illustrations (see page 96)
taken from *Conoscerti, Enciclopedia dei Test*
© 1986 Gruppo Editoriale Fabbri SpA, Milan

Introductions by Jane Lyle

© 1989 Translation, remaining text and design, The Hamlyn Publishing Group Limited,
a division of The Octopus Publishing Group,
Michelin House, 81 Fulham Road, London, U.K.

This 1989 edition published by Crescent Books,
distributed by Crown Publishers, Inc., 225 Park Avenue South,
New York, New York 10003.

Produced by Mandarin Offset
Printed and bound in Hong Kong

ISBN 0-517-679280
hgfedcba

Contents

Introduction

The magical, mysterious land of dreams is one we all visit every night – whether or not we remember our experiences. This unseeen and puzzling world has intrigued both scientists and mystics for thousands of years. But, despite numerous theories, the answer to the question 'Why do we dream?' still eludes the most eminent researchers.

Approximately every ninety minutes during the night we enter a period of light sleep. This may last just a few seconds, or continue for as long as twenty minutes. This is when we dream.

Serious sleep research began in America in the 1950s, and soon spread to specially-designed sleep laboratories all over the world. By attaching tiny electrodes to volunteers' faces and scalps, scientists were able to measure brain-wave activity and other physical cycles that rose and fell throughout the night. One of their earliest discoveries was that the eyes – even of blind people — move about rapidly beneath closed lids during a dream. They established this by waking their subjects at intervals – and found that if they woke them during REM, or Rapid Eye Movement, periods the volunteers reported dreams.

Further experiments have established that dreams are essential to mental and physical well-being – for when people have been deliberately denied dream-sleep they soon become quite disturbed, experiencing hallucinations and a range of psychotic symptoms.

Designing dreams

Another scientific discovery concerns the deliberate manipulation of dreams – something magicians in many cultures have been aware of for centuries. One major experiment took place in Edinburgh, where student volunteers were played a selection of names while they slept. Subjects were woken from REM periods of sleep and asked to describe their dreams. In a remarkably high number of cases these names appeared to penetrate the dreaming mind, producing some interesting examples of how the subconscious often translates things literally – or creates surprising images.

Another form of dream manipulation comes from the Temiar tribe in Malaysia. These people have always known about the importance of dreams and teach their children to confront nightmare figures. In this way, they say, the children will be free from evil spirits once they reach adulthood. They also regularly share their dreams, believing that dreams can predict the future. Forewarned is forearmed, and so they are able to avoid potential problems or deal with them before they get out of hand.

Lucid dreams – where the dreamer is fully aware he or she is dreaming – are currently under investigation, too. Prompted by mystics like Don Juan, made famous through the books of Carlos Castaneda, lucid dreams have entered the laboratory. Don Juan maintains that by learning how to control your dreams you can increase psychic powers and creativity. One British scientist, Dr Keith Hearne, believes that such dreams represent an extraordinary reservoir of untapped mental abilities, and can be deliberately encouraged.

Sleeping on it

Indeed, creativity and problem-solving are two of the most fascinating aspects of dreams, for many famous people have been directly inspired by them. Niels Bohr (1885–1962) owed his Nobel Prize to a combination of hard work plus an inspired dream. He was working on the structure of the atom, and was finding it almost impossible to visualize his ideas. But one night he had a vivid dream in which he found himself standing right in the middle of a brightly-burning sun. He looked up, and saw planets – attached to the sun by slender threads – revolving around the central body where he stood. Suddenly, the hot, gaseous sun began to cool and the whole whirling image came to a solid standstill. Bohr used the analogy of a solar system to describe vividly how electrons revolve around a nucleus – and won the prestigious prize for his concept.

Creative dreaming

Since many dreams contain the seeds of a story, you might expect writers to be inspired by them – and many authors have openly admitted creative help from the unconscious. Robert Louis Stevenson was a great dreamer, although he did not always enjoy his experiences. His famous horror-story, *Dr Jekyll and Mr Hyde*, came to him in a dream.

Music, too, has benefited from dreams. 'You are going to hear a dream, a dream that I have made sound . . . I dreamed all this; never could my poor head have invented such a thing purposely,' wrote Wagner in a letter to a friend. He was referring to his opera, *Tristan und Isolde*. Similarly, Giuseppe Tartini, the Italian composer, described how he dreamed of selling his soul to the devil, and gave him his violin to see how he would play. The devil turned out to be a talented musician, and exquisitely beautiful music filled Tartini's dream. The resulting sonata, which he claimed was a pale imitation of the dream music, was *The Devil's Trill*.

Priests and prophets

References to dreams are found throughout ancient literature, whether carved on the walls of Egyptian temples, in the Bible, or in what is thought to be the oldest dream book of all, compiled by Artemidorus of Ephesus in the second century AD. Dream messages were taken very seriously, and every civilized country in the Ancient World had its own interpreters, or soothsayers. The Ancient Greeks believed that dreams entered the sleeping mind through what were called the Gates of Dreams. One gate was made of horn, the other of ivory – prophetic dreams came through the horn gate, while warnings came through the ivory gate. With the help of special priests and priestesses, the Ancient Greeks searched their dreams for divinely inspired messages.

Those who were troubled or sick would visit a sacred shrine, such as

Asclepius' temple on Kos. Rituals were performed invoking the god or goddess of the temple, and then the visitors would sleep in a special sanctuary, in the hope of receiving help in their dreams. These were then analysed by the priests. Sometimes they contained details of herbal remedies, and practical advice. In other dreams, the sick person received a visit from the god – and woke in the best of health.

Dreams of the future

Although many twentieth-century psychoanalysts have dismissed the idea of prophetic dreams, they do happen – and they do come true. John Godley, who became Lord Kilbracken, had an amazing series of dreams over twelve years, which predicted the winners of horse races. Since he shared these supernatural tips with friends, his successes are well-documented, and he became famous in the 1950s as a psychic punter, working as racing correspondent for the *Daily Mirror*.

Other predictive dreams contain warnings, and in many cases have saved the lives of those who paid attention to them. In April 1973, for example, a terrible tragedy devastated four Somerset villages. The local Ladies' Guild had chartered a plane to take them to Switzerland for a day trip. Severe weather conditions near Basle caused their plane to crash, with the loss of more than one hundred lives. Yet one woman, who had booked to go, returned her ticket and stayed at home because of a dream in which there was a terrible snowstorm and the plane she was in crashed into some trees. The bodies of her friends lay close to the wreckage, and this is exactly what happened in reality.

How to make sense of your dreams

With a little effort, you can become your own expert dream interpreter. For you create your dreams, and while you sleep you become an artist, author and composer of them. By getting closer in touch with the dreamer within you, you will see yourself, and others, in a new light.

The first step is to keep a regular dream diary. Immediately you wake, scribble down everything you can possibly remember about your dreams. At first, this may simply be an assortment of vague feelings, colours and, perhaps, some images. Some people can recall only a word or a name, and on some mornings there may be nothing to record at all. But the more you practise, the more you are likely to remember. If you persevere, you should soon be writing down detailed descriptions.

Analysing your dreams takes intuition. First of all, you must ask yourself how you feel on waking – happy and relaxed, depressed, filled with foreboding, or confused? Your mood is an important key to the meaning of your dream, for the same symbol can contain both positive and negative messages and must always be interpreted in context.

Spend a little time thinking about whether the dream is simply a scene from real life, or whether it has a deeper, veiled meaning. 'Real' dreams are one of the mind's safety valves, and are showing you some actual event or relationship which may have upset you – either in the distant past, or in your present life. Such dreams are valuable friends, often shedding fresh light on your problems by revealing things your conscious mind has forgotten or is unaware of.

Highly imaginative dreams filled with bizarre symbols, fantastic creatures and mystical themes are just as practical, too – although it may take more thought to make sense of them in the cold light of day. Using a dreamer's dictionary like this can help you by uncovering hidden meanings, or simply by stimulating your imagination.

Dream work

Once you have established a firm link between your waking mind and your dreams, you are ready to try problem-solving while you sleep. This does not always work, mainly because we forget our night thoughts so rapidly. However, when it does work, results can be spectacular.

Simply relax, settle down in bed and think as clearly as you can about whatever it is that is worrying you. Do not even attempt to solve a problem consciously, just mentally list all the aspects or, if you prefer, write them down. Then, in your own words, ask your subsconcious, higher self or God to send you a helpful, enlightening dream.

It is also a good idea to ask for a clear dream, which you will remember when you wake up next morning. Calmly tell yourself that you are ready to receive this information, and fully expect an answer to your question. Finally, go to sleep. Naturally, problem-solving during sleep is a skill like any other, and needs practise. However, the results of your repeated efforts will be intriguing and rewarding.

1
Sensations

Everyone has physical dreams. During these dreams you may experience very real sensations, such as biting or itching. Disembodied voices may speak to you, or you could find yourself soaring weightlessly over rooftops. Hippocrates, the famous Greek philosopher and father of medicine, said, 'Some dreams are divinely inspired but others are the direct result of the physical body'. Modern research into the fields of psychology, physiology and the paranormal seems to come close to agreeing with him.

When we fall asleep, our active, day-time self is unconscious – but still capable of responding to outside stimulii. Once we have entered the dream state, or Rapid Eye Movement stage of sleep, our bodies are remarkably active. This extraordinary flickering movement of the eyes takes place beneath closed lids – accompanied by other physical changes including irregular breathing, increased heart-rate, and blood rushing to the brain. In addition, we lose muscle tone all over the body. This, it is thought, accounts for very real feelings of paralysis in dreams, as part of the mind becomes aware that it cannot move normally.

Memories
Memories of babyhood – long forgotten by the conscious mind – can also arise in our dreams as sensations. Babies' senses are incredibly clear, for they are free from years of absorbing information. Dreams involving colour are highly symbolic, and may be harking back to the first colours you ever saw – and the sensations that went with them.

The commonly-experienced sensation of flying is a mystery to interpreters of dreams. Psychologists call it depersonalization and others say it is a race-memory going back to the dawn of time when we inhabited the seas or were airborne creatures. Mystics maintain that we are actually flying in all our dreams, when the astral body leaves the physical one at night and goes travelling.

Sensations

Biting
This dream often indicates a highly-strung personality, possibly frustrated in its ideals, with a tendency to regard the future with considerable trepidation. Biting into a piece of bread, on the other hand, shows some kind of threat to those nearest and dearest to you. Biting into fruit is a sign of tact and diplomacy. Biting someone else shows that arguments and lies may disturb your relationship with your partner, despite both of you declaring your love.

Blindness
Going blind yourself shows that a lover may be in some kind of danger from someone else and suggests that there may be disappointment in love on the way. Dreaming about a blind person asking for money is a warning to be cautious in something you are involved in, and a blind person with a guide dog is a bringer of interesting news.

Climbing
Climbing a mountain in a dream suggests that you have worries and preoccupations which seem to be insurmountable, but it is more than likely that you are exaggerating their importance. If you try to reassert the calm, clear-headed side of your nature, you will see everything starting to turn out for the good. Climbing a ladder indicates that you are ascending the ladder of

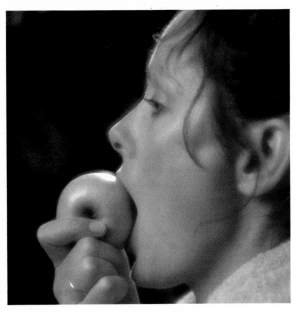

Tact is signalled by biting into fruit in a dream

business success, and is thus a favourable sign – so long as you do not set your sights unrealistically high. Seeing a climbing plant such as ivy or runner beans in your dream suggests long-lasting, faithful friendships: do not be discouraged by any minor hiccups in these relationships.

Darkness
If you find yourself in darkness in your dream – for example in a cave or a tunnel – there may be a major emotional upset on the way in which your inner strength and outward decision-making ability will be tested to the full. But if you manage to escape from the darkness back into the sunlight, this promises success in your work and happiness in love. Fear of the dark in a dream suggests that you have very major obstacles to overcome in your life. A dark or shadowy person or thing you cannot quite identify indicates a subconscious fear that needs to be brought out into the open and rationalized. Someone being kept in the dark, figuratively or literally, means that relationships with your loved one, or someone close to you, may be difficult.

Deafness
Being deaf in a dream is not a particularly good sign. There is news on the way which you will not like and which may leave you depressed. A dream about trying to make yourself understood to a deaf person means you are deluding yourself in matters of love.

Drunk
Seeing someone drunk in a pub in a dream shows that you are in poor physical condition. Getting drunk yourself indicates that small gains are heading your way. To dream of a drunk in the street suggests careless spending on your part, while seeing a drunk lying on the ground means your health may be at risk. A sleeping drunk is a symbol of your excessively hard work, while to dream of a drunk who is singing indicates that you have little confidence in your abilities. Getting 'high' or 'drunk' on a piece of music, a sunset, a painting or something similar in a dream indicates that you are highly sensitive.

Echo
Dreaming about an echo indicates that you will receive a favourable response to a proposal, either from a would-be lover who is proving elusive or, less romantically, from a business acquaintance.

Falling
This is one of the most frequent experiences in dreams. It indicates some kind of loss, especially in love or money

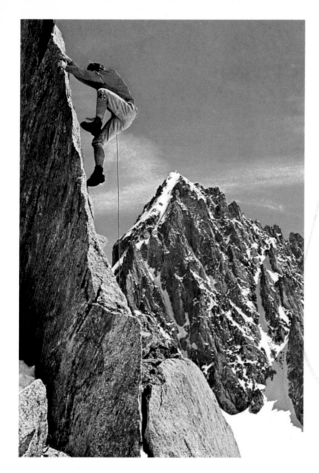

Mountain-climbing in a dream means exaggerated worries

Growing taller
Someone else growing taller in a dream indicates a fear of what the future may have in store, but you yourself growing shows that your self-confidence and self-respect are increasing daily. A house or other building growing taller means that financial improvements are on the way, and a plant or tree increasing in height also suggests a forthcoming state of prosperity.

Itching and scratching
Itchy feet in dreams, as one might expect, signify a yearning for new opportunities and new places to live; itching hands indicate that money is on the way. If your nose itches, you should be careful because you are at a stage in your work where you could easily make mistakes, and you should therefore think very carefully before you do anything that might jeopardise your position.

Scratching oneself in a dream normally indicates inner insecurity and lack of satisfaction. Scratching your face reflects a temporary setback, and scratching your hands suggests you are perhaps being unfaithful in a relationship. Scratching your legs means you have serious doubts about something, but if the dream involves scratching your head, an unexpected boost to your spirits is indicated.

Profit of some kind is in the offing if you dream of floating

matters. If you dream of falling out of bed, this indicates that you are highly sensitive to your environment and the behaviour of others, while falling into something unpleasant, such as a dung-heap, indicates new prospects at work.

Floating
A large area of water in a dream usually signifies danger of some kind. However, a much more favourable sign is if someone or something is floating on the water, because it indicates that you will overcome future obstacles. It can also herald success and major financial or other gains.

Flying
Flying is one of the most common sensations in dreams and it can have various meanings. Flying across the sea means you are far too conceited and confident for your own good, while flying over an abyss means insufferable, annoying behaviour on your part. Flying at a very low level indicates setbacks in love.

Mood
Paradoxically, being in a good mood in a dream suggests that you are tired and unhappy in real life; you should try not to get too wrapped up in yourself and try not to be so difficult with your partner. If you dream about being in a bad mood, you can expect major problems involving the law in some way.

Noise
If you dream about children making a noise outside your

A nude woman suggests the dreamer is under stress

roars in your dream, you will lose or waste a substantial amount of money, but if the roar is made by water, you will have an unpleasant experience connected with the opposite sex.

Nudity
This very common theme in dreams is primarily an ill omen; if you dream about walking around nude, you are having quite severe emotional problems, possibly due to a failure at work, while sleeping in the nude means you may be cheated by someone you thought you could trust. Seeing someone else naked means you are anxious about the welfare of somebody. If it is a man you see naked, there will be setbacks in your relationship with your partner; and if it is a woman, you are under stress.

Pain
Any dream involving pain indicates that you are experiencing small, short-lived problems and irritations. If your eyes hurt in the dream, it is because someone in your family is ill or off-colour; an earache heralds the arrival of unwelcome news and a headache means that for a while things will go against you to a certain extent.

Peace
Feeling at peace with yourself and others in your dream means that you are quite the opposite in real life: you are being plagued by doubts and suspicions which will take a long time to go away. A period of peace after anything from a minor quarrel to a major war in a dream means that you are entertaining impossible, unrealizable hopes. Peace which is broken, perhaps by a loud noise, indicates anger.

Pinch
Pinching someone else in your dream indicates that your mood at the moment is a confused, distracted one and you are finding it hard to keep things in proportion. You should try to sit back and calm down, as you have weighty problems to face up to which can only be solved by a calm, rational approach. If someone else pinches you, the indications are that your health is going to suffer, but you can lessen the impact of the illness, or even avoid it altogether, if you look after yourself properly.

Pregnancy
Dreaming that you are pregnant suggests that you are going through a hard time. If a girl dreams about being pregnant, she will have no trouble surmounting her various problems because of help from other people, but if an older woman dreams she is pregnant she needs to be very patient before she can achieve her aims and ambitions. Strangely enough, it is not at all unusual for a man to dream he is pregnant: it also suggests he needs to fight long and hard to achieve the success he is hoping for.

house, you should keep your cool and be patient while waiting for the news you are eagerly expecting. Any noise at night in a dream means you need much more rest and relaxation than you are getting, but traffic noise indicates success in your career.

Hearing a person or an animal roaring in a dream is not a good sign; there is an unpleasant surprise in store which will upset you more than you might expect it to. If the wind

Remembering

Remembering a promise in a dream means you are being too obstinate; while remembering a birthday demonstrates that in your real life you are showing over-sensitive behaviour caused by an unanticipated disappointment connected with someone of the opposite sex. If you remember somebody's name in a dream, you are feeling very lively and very much in control of the way your life is going; remembering a debt owed to you means a short period of dissatisfaction and unhappiness. Remembering money that you owe someone else means there are contacts to be taken up again after a long absence.

Repulsion

Dreaming of a man who is repulsive signifies a financial venture going decidedly wrong, and a repulsive woman suggests that things are reaching a crisis point in your life. A repulsive old man means slow but constant progress in your career. If you find the food you are eating in your dream repulsive, it is because you are about to get involved in painful arguments with your partner; if something you smell is disgusting, it means you will be the object of criticism and slander.

Resting

In dreams, as in real life, working for long periods without having a rest inevitably leads to physical and mental stress: you should try to find new interests to stimulate your mind and lead you away from this over-zealous preoccupation, or there is a chance you may lose your job by wearing yourself down. Resting in an armchair in a dream shows that a difficult situation is just around the corner, while taking a quick nap on a bed means that you feel confident in yourself and have a sense of responsibility.

Reviving

Reviving someone who is unconscious in a dream means you have been placed in a very responsible position at work; if they were near death before you tried to revive them, it shows you are being careful and considerate in your actions; and if they were drowning, you are lively and full of initiative. Resuscitating a child means you are sensible and intelligent. If it is a man who is being revived, you need to put right an error made in your work before it produces repercussions, and if it is a woman, you will be involved in an argument about money.

Seeing

To dream of seeing something but not being able to tell what it is suggests you need to clear up a complicated situation before it gets even worse. Seeing something in the distance but not being able to reach it indicates that your plans for the future may be over-ambitious and you should scale them down to achievable proportions.

A difficult situation looms if you dream about resting

Sleep

It is quite common to dream about seeing yourself sleep or seeing someone else sleep. If it is a restless sleep, your health is less than perfect at the moment, but if it is a deep sleep, it indicates that you will make new business connections. If you dream about waking up after a long sleep, you are likely to be full of energy and vitality. Sleeping with someone else in a dream means you are both optimistic and trusting.

Smell

Sensations are often felt even more vividly in dreams than they are in everyday life, and this is equally true of smells. A strong smell means new friendships are coming which will stand you in good stead in the future, but a more delicate one means bad advice is being given to you which should not be accepted.

An unpleasant smell is a warning that you should take more care of yourself: you are taking on too much responsibility and working too hard. A pleasant smell such as that of perfume signals an estrangement from a colleague at work or from someone who is not doing you any good is imminent, while an odour of flowers means disorder and chaos in your life. The smell of alcohol signifies intense but short-lived pleasure and an inevitable aftermath of regret.

Touching an animal in a dream means you enjoy good health

Stumbling

If you fall over in the street in your dream, it might be a good idea to put off making an important decision for the time being. Stumbling on a flight of stairs suggests that you have a distorted view of things, and tripping over a stone indicates obstacles are looming that need to be avoided and that you will make costly mistakes.

Touching

Touching a man in a dream signifies that you are keeping promises, while touching a woman reveals your need to be more flexible. Touching a child indicates both a sense of responsibility and a state of mental poise and tranquillity. Touching an animal suggests you are in good health and can expect to stay that way for a long time to come.

Vision

Dreaming about having a vision – seeing a ghost, for example – is not normally a favourable sign. It reflects a vain, selfish personality which is unsociable and unenthusiastic about everything: unless you can do something about this aspect of your character, it will lead to some unpleasant consequences in your social and emotional life.

Voice

A high voice in a dream indicates that you are temporarily in a bad mood, while a softly-spoken person, paradoxically, indicates that you are harbouring aggressive intentions. A loud voice heralds a period of happiness, and a nasal voice suggests that you might have ridiculous pretensions. If someone speaks with a gruff or hoarse voice, it means you are being too hurried in making a decision. If you hear your own voice in a dream it suggests that you should be careful not to make any false moves, because they could be very harmful to your career at this time. Losing your voice in a dream means you are wasting time gossiping.

Dreaming of deep sleep presages fresh business connections

Colours

If you dream of a red car, you may be finding life dull and want to put some pep into it

Green

Dreaming about a green field suggests that a welcome invitation may be in prospect; green cloth signifies projects which you are enthusiastic about. Green clothes in a dream indicate your involvement in long and complicated negotiations or discussions, and a green plant signifies that you have gained well-deserved recognition. Green, damp wood means you are being too extravagant and letting your imagination run away with you.

Red and Blue

Two of the colours which appear in dreams and are most often remembered are red and blue. Both have a very precise meaning, both in popular tradition and also in the light of what modern psychology has told us about the human mind.

Red is a symbol of aggression. This is not necessarily a negative characteristic: in fact it can have a very positive meaning, suggesting that you have a need to make your mark on the world rather than letting others take the lead and instead of being lazy and afraid of facing up to problems. So dreaming in red often means vitality, a desire to act, be positive and get things done. Statistically, it has been shown that women dream in red more often than men do.

Dreaming of red clothes of any kind indicates passion and sensitivity in emotional relationships; a red thread means a desperate need for love and affection; and a red pencil or crayon an ability to support and sustain others in their hour of need. A red car or other vehicle reflects a craving for novel and interesting things to happen.

Blue reflects a feeling of contentment and a need for peace and tranquillity. A person who often dreams in blue, or about blue things, is likely to be generous, understanding of others, and someone who will help his fellow humans, without expecting a reward for doing so. The colour blue also indicates a forceful but balanced personality.

Paradoxically, then, red and blue are colours which complement each other in dreams, one appearing as the other disappears, for most people have the characteristics represented by both colours.

2
Emotions

Waking or sleeping, your emotions are powerful forces. When they enter your dreams, they can often seem even more intense than usual. So when you are puzzling over the meaning of an emotional dream, you must be honest with yourself about your own emotional state – for this can profoundly influence your dreams.

A team of American psychiatrists conducted an interesting experiment to see if depression was revealed in dreams. They collected written reports of dreams from a group of seriously depressed people, and mixed these with the same number of dream descriptions from normal people. When they gave these documents to an independent psychiatrist, he was able to separate the reports accurately. Depressed dreams, it seems, are filled with failure and negativity.

Our sexuality also emerges in dreams – but not to the extent Sigmund Freud (1856–1939), father of modern psychoanalysis, believed. Modern research into the mood-altering chemicals produced by the body has shown that, to a great extent, sex is all in the mind. Hormone levels affect our sex drive, triggering certain centres in the brain. Even animals have sexy dreams!

If we are frustrated in our daily lives we are more likely to have erotic dreams as some kind of compensation. Another explanation is that we are mentally trying out a potential partner, or are very attracted to them but consciously unaware of this.

Anger and anxiety are also commonly dealt with while we are asleep – although apparently insoluble problems can equally cause insomnia and broken nights. Deeply repressed anger may even have triggered some extraordinary murder cases, for there are a number of instances where people have won a verdict of 'Not Guilty' because they have been able to prove that they killed their spouse whilst dreaming.

Emotions

Admiration
This is a good subject to dream about. If you are admiring someone else, this is a sign that your partner is genuinely in love with you; if the dream is about someone admiring you, you have many friends that respect you a great deal.

Anxiety
Despite what one might think, being anxious in a dream is actually a sign that your frequent disquiet and worry is unjustified and something you expect to fail will in fact succeed, proving your anxiety unfounded.

Calm
Calm after a storm or other major event in a dream shows an end to worries and a period of peace and quiet after rows and disagreements. But if the dream involves a calm sea, it is a warning that you may be at risk from some kind of snare or ambush lying beneath the surface of an apparently innocent situation. Dreaming about someone who is calm in the face of a stressful situation indicates that you are an unflappable, reflective type of person.

A calm sea in a dream may carry a warning

Concern
This concern may be directed towards your mother, and if so it betrays a certain amount of nervousness and irritability which you need to keep under a tight rein. If it is your father you are concerned about, you are hard-working and scrupulous in your dealings with others. Concern about a son or daughter means that there are agreements to be reached within a project which has important financial implications. If you are worried about someone's health, there will be family tensions, while if you are afraid about the future, you have shyness to overcome.

Embarrassment
Being embarrassed in a dream indicates that you must put forward concrete proposals where these are required at work, while embarrassing someone else means that negotiations which you are undertaking are now coming to an advantageous conclusion. Being embarrassed by the generosity of others in your dreams means you are an intelligent, practically-minded person.

Envy
Envying someone in a dream actually means that you respect, or even love, that person. Likewise, if in the dream someone else envies you it means that others appreciate and respect you in real life.

Guilt
Dreaming about being guilty of some misdeed is not necessarily an ill omen; more often than not it reflects improving prospects. Dreaming about other people being found guilty of something wrong indicates – if it is a man doing the dreaming – unusual or unaccustomed situations, while if it is a woman, it indicates unusual over-sensitivity and intolerance.

Humiliation
A man being humiliated in your dream indicates an important decision which is likely to change your emotional situation in a big way. A humiliated woman suggests good relationships within your family.

Hysteria
Dreaming about someone who is hysterical means you should take care not to be forced into anything against your will, while if it is you having hysterics, it indicates that you should follow the advice of someone close to you.

Outrage
Being outraged by something in a dream shows you are about to take a major step forward in your work, and doing something outrageous, possibly offending other people, means that you are still finding it hard to get over the dislike you feel for a former friend.

Pity
Feeling pity for someone or something shows an unusual level of confidence and decisiveness which will help you

over obstacles at work that normally you might not be able to deal with. If someone you know expresses pity for you in your dream, attractive opportunities are being opened up for you at work, but they could also be risky or hazardous and you should be careful not to make any false moves or be over-eager to take them up. Asking for someone's pity in a dream indicates a sizeable amount of money coming in, and success in the field of romance.

Pride
This is one of the few dreams which reflects exactly what is going on in reality: it means that you are being selfish and ambitious, and creating yourself enemies in the process. Unless you mend your ways, you will very soon suffer the consequences. If a woman dreams of being excessively proud it symbolizes the arrival of sad or worrying news, while if the dreamer is a man it shows that your relations with other people are rather superficial. If the pride is justified in the particular circumstances, on the other hand, perhaps on account of a special achievement, it suggests you are having an agonizing wait for something or someone in real life.

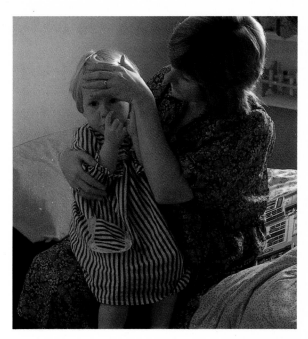

Finances are at stake if concern in a dream is for your daughter

Dreaming of someone in a rage signals future unhappiness

Rage
Dreaming of anyone showing rage is generally not a sign of good fortune: it indicates some future unhappiness verging on desperation, caused by a disappointment you had not expected from someone you loved. If you dream of going into a rage with a friend because of what he or she has done, you are starting to worry too much about the health of a person close to you when it is already on the mend. If someone else goes into a rage at you, it is a foretaste of unpleasant news to come.

Shame
Being ashamed in a dream indicates a bumpy emotional life, which could be damaging in the long term. However, if someone else is ashamed of themselves in a dream, it means that you have planned great goals for the future.

Shyness
Dreaming of a shy man indicates a lively discussion with someone at work; while the appearance of a shy woman reveals your uncertainty and doubt relating to someone you love.

If it is an old person being shy, you should take the advice of others into account when deciding how to get round a major obstacle at work. If it is someone else being shy in your dream, it indicates you have a low level of confidence in your own abilities, but if it is you that is being shy, there is a period of despondency on the way.

Behaviour

Arguing

An argument in a dream suggests one in real life: disputes, business problems and a possible break with a loved one. A personal dispute or disagreement indicates you are in a combative frame of mind and are taking things out on other people.

Dreaming about a legal dispute shows you are agitated and dissatisfied at present, but others are not aware of this fact. A union dispute suggests immoderate behaviour and lack of responsibility on your part.

Cheating at cards in a dream can be a bad sign in real life

Interrogating

If you interrogate someone else in your dream in an attempt to find out the truth, it suggests you are not good at forming lasting relationships with people around you. If it is you that is being interrogated, there is a pleasant surprise, involving a journey, in the offing.

Justifying yourself

This is a dream which reflects inner conflicts, a difficult personality, and disappointing experiences. No matter what you are trying to justify, or who you are doing the explaining to, your outlook is one of unhappiness.

Lying

Lying to your parents in a dream indicates that you are involved in a friendship which is doing you more harm than good: lying to a friend indicates concealed hatred of someone; lying to your loved one, suggests that you have differences of opinion with them which will be easily resolved and lying to someone you work for means that a worrying piece of news connected with work is on its way.

Falsifying or forging documents, money or someone's signature in a dream is a sign of major difficulties ahead.

Cheating someone else, or pretending to have feelings that you do not in fact have, is a bad sign in a dream: it suggests you are worried about a project you have a particular interest in and it is more than likely you will not achieve what you hope for. If you cheat at a game of cards or sporting activity, it means you are not acting consistently and risk losing the trust or affection of your partner.

Swindling has the same bad results in a dream as it does in real life: a man being swindled indicates that you are undertaking a very risky venture, and a woman being

Try not to end up with one in the eye if you fight in a dream

Fight

Taking part in a fight in your dreams suggests you have many enemies, but if you emerge victorious it reflects the fact that they are powerless to do anything against you. Getting stabbed in a fight symbolizes failure. Being in a fight is an unfavourable dream for anyone in business, travelling, or in love.

Forbidding

Dreaming of forbidding a meeting to take place indicates that you need to be more flexible and adaptable, while to dream of banning a procession suggests that you have confused ideas. Forbidding or sabotaging a hunt meeting in a dream will bring you good luck and an upturn in your business affairs. If you forbid a relation to get married in a dream, you are entering an uncertain and prickly period from an emotional point of view.

Happy and sad dreams

Happy dreams

Quite simply, joy in a dream means joy in your everyday life: it indicates good health and success in everything you do.

A man laughing in a dream is a symbol of new knowledge or skills gained from a new project at work, while a woman laughing symbolizes your introversion and unsociability. A child's laughter means pleasant news from a long way away. If something you do or say in your dream makes other people laugh, you need to face up to some fundamental differences between you and your partner.

Sad dreams

Crying with sadness actually indicates overcoming an obstacle, a good financial position and success in love. Crying with happiness indicates anxiety and arguments. Weeping with rage indicates malicious gossip by people close to you. Weeping in torrents means that you will learn that somebody loves you, when this was quite unexpected on your part.

In general, a dream where someone else is crying means you are letting yourself be panicked unnecessarily. More specifically, a woman crying is an indication that you need to take extra care in things you are involved in, while a baby crying suggests there may be significant improvements in your domestic situation in the near future.

As is often the case when death or misfortune occur in dreams, mourning is, paradoxically, not a sign of bereavement in real life. Wearing mourning dress in a dream foreshadows an unexpected but very happy event, and dreaming that your family is in mourning suggests that the dreamer has abilities and qualities which bode well career-wise and emotionally.

Generally speaking, being unhappy in a dream indicates, paradoxically, that you have put your unhappiness behind you in real life. Indeed, the more unhappy you are in the dream, the more happy you can expect to be in reality.

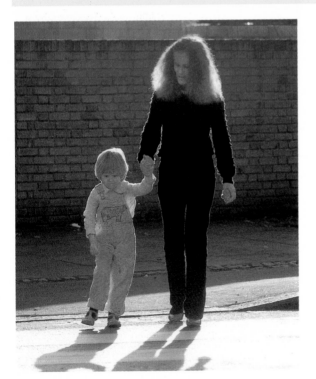

Obeying your parents in a dream is good news for your partner

swindled shows that your behaviour at the moment may be intemperate and foolhardy. If you dream about swindling a customer, there will be unpleasant gossip directed at you.

Obeying

Obeying your own parents in a dream means you have profound and genuine feelings about your partner; obeying someone at work shows that your plans within your job are slowing down and you are worried about the possibility of running out of steam.

Rebuking

If the rebuke you make in the dream is a justified one, it signifies that you have found a clever solution to an emotional problem, but if it is unjustified, it heralds a minor but unpleasant period of unhappiness or illness. If you justifiably rebuke your son or daughter, your prospects at work have never been better than they are at the moment.

If unjustified, reprimanding your children for something they have done in a dream indicates professional difficulties, and giving your husband or wife a ticking-off means that you need to keep an eye on how much money you are spending. Reprimanding any other relative means you are behaving in a confused and uncertain way at the moment. Reproving a man in a dream means you should be able to profit from a very favourable opportunity which is going to be given to you.

Love

Abandonment
Dreaming about abandoning someone is an unfavourable sign: it means the loss of a friendship or a loved one whom you relied upon. Dreaming about being abandoned yourself means problems on the horizon.

Adultery
Any dream about committing adultery shows problems in your love life; you are likely to be undergoing traumas and may be frequently at your wits' end. If you resist the temptation, however, it is a sign of a contented existence guided by common sense and strong principles.

Bride
A bride at the altar presages good news in almost everything you do; but if she is on her own, without a bridegroom, your health is at slight risk. If you find yourself standing beside the bride at the altar, a desire you have been nurturing for a long time will soon come to fruition.

Caress
Caressing a child is a sign that doubts need to be cleared up as soon as possible, while caressing a husband, wife or other loved one suggests an important piece of business which is gradually slipping away from you.

Divorce
This dream in fact means the opposite of what one might expect. If a married person dreams about getting divorced, it usually indicates that his or her marriage is a strong one, without the jealousy and unfaithfulness of some marriages.

Embrace
The exact meaning of this dream depends more on the person being embraced than the action itself, though to dream of an embrace shows that you are being open and receptive. Embracing a friend indicates that pleasant news is on the way, but embracing an enemy is a sign of betrayal. Embracing members of your family means that you will shortly be told a secret which you must not disclose.

Groom
Marriage is one of the last rituals we all take seriously. So if you dream of a groom – unless you are about to go to a wedding, or be married – it is a symbol. A groom standing at the altar means a sacrifice will have to be made to obtain your heart's desire. When a man sees a groom in his dreams it means he is about to make an important commitment. For a woman it indicates she is secretly ambitious, and should devote more time to her career.

Husband
If a woman dreams she has a husband when in real life she is not married, it indicates that she is not yet ready to get involved in relationships which tie her down in any way, while if she is married and dreams about her husband, marital quarrels are in the offing. Dreaming about someone else's husband suggests that you may show a lack of seriousness about important matters, though if you are not married yourself it indicates that a meaningful and lasting relationship is in prospect.

Infidelity
If you dream that either a friend, or your partner, is being unfaithful to you, there is no cause for alarm: it actually

Two happy lovers in a dream herald romance

indicates quite the opposite. But if you dream about being unfaithful yourself, there are very strong temptations in your path, so you should get ready to resist them.

Jealousy

The appearance of jealousy in a dream is a sign of worry and anxiety. Being jealous yourself means happiness in matters of the heart, while being the cause of jealousy means you are repressing emotions. Dreaming about being jealous of someone at work means setbacks in love.

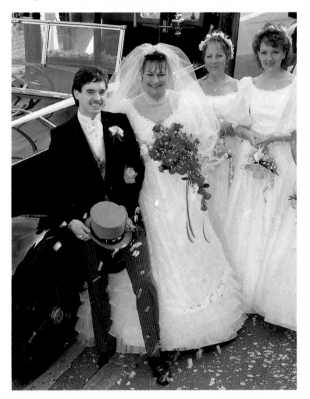

Going to a wedding means there is good news on the way

Kiss

This usually symbolizes happiness in dreams. Kissing someone means the emergence of a new love affair, while being kissed by your own partner indicates sincerity and genuineness in the relationship. Kissing a dead person is a sign of a long and happy life.

Living together

Living together can often cause difficulties in real life, and the same is true in dreams. Any dream involving living with someone of the opposite sex is a danger signal: someone is making excessive demands on your time and emotions. Sharing a home with someone of the same sex, however,

indicates that you are heading for a possible deception in love, and if you dream of sharing with someone you do not know, you will soon have to confront many different problems – which may not necessarily be emotional ones.

Love

Dreaming about falling in love means that someone loves you, and will tell you so very soon. If you dream about love passing you by, it in fact means that you are shortly to fall in love and get married. This is another dream which indicates the opposite of what you might expect.

Lovers

Dreaming about two happy lovers heralds new experiences involving the opposite sex, and a lovers' tiff foretells harmony with a partner. Dreaming about being attracted to your own partner means you are faithful to each other, but if he or she is pale and unhappy, there is the chance of one of you succumbing to an affair with someone else.

Marriage

Dreaming about a marriage is not the happy omen it might seem to be: if you are the one getting married, it indicates resentment and friction with someone which will last for a long time; there will also be a major financial loss which will have a bad effect on your living standards and may also adversely affect your health. Going to someone else's wedding means there is good news on the way.

Getting married because you love someone in a dream shows an enthusiastic approach to a new project at work, while being forced to get married against your will, for example in an arranged marriage, signifies that you can look forward to a lively and eventful period in real life. Marrying someone for their money means you are behaving nervously and irritably. A secret marriage suggests you are very uncertain and confused because of a disappointment in love.

Remarrying

Remarrying someone who is younger than you in a dream indicates that you are facing a delicate situation which needs to be handled carefully, but getting remarried to someone older means you often feel tired and over-stressed. Getting married to a widow or widower is a danger signal in a dream: you are taking on too many burdens at work, and there is a serious risk of your overdoing things unless you sit back and take things a little easier.

Wife

If you dream about your own wife, it suggests there will be arguments and jealousy between you which can only be overcome by your being patient and caring. If you are not married and you dream about having a wife, it shows you are not ready for a long-term relationship.

3
Actions

Dreams filled with action are frequently symbolic. Many of these symbols are directly connected to popular phrases and sayings which the subconscious translates into its own language.

Take cleaning, for example – we say 'I'm going to make a clean start', or refer to a successful business as 'cleaning up', meaning it is making a lot of money easily and quickly. Clean also means completely, as in 'I clean forgot', or 'they cleaned me out'. Once you start to look for parallels you will soon be able to spot all kinds of double, or even triple, meanings in your dreams.

There are two further major kinds of action dream – literal dreams, and action-replay dreams. Literal dreams are completely free from symbolism or imagination, for they represent a straightforward message from the subconscious. These messages attempt to bring something to your attention in the most obvious possible way, and often focus on something you have forgotten or overlooked. They can also present problem-solving solutions, suggest new ways of doing things or give you creative ideas. Sometimes they are a kind of wish-fulfillment – a dream trying to come true, if only in fantasy.

Other action dreams seem to be identical replays of situations you have already lived through. These dreams are trying to help you come to terms with an event in the past which you may have misinterpreted. By dreaming of your actions, your mind is giving you an opportunity to set the memory records straight – and fully understand a situation. At one time scientists believed all our dreams were a way of filing information in the memory banks, but have now realized that dreams are much more complex and mysterious than that.

Actions

Arresting
This is a classic example of a dream which means its opposite: freedom of action and behaviour.

Bathing
Actually getting into a bath or a pool of water of any kind, as opposed to looking at it, shows that you are a person who likes to get involved in situations rather than observing them from afar; the water, though, may be much deeper than it looks, so you should take care and assess its depth before you leap in.

Breaking something
Breaking plates in a dream is a token of great material well-being, and breaking cups or glasses indicates generosity and enthusiasm. Breaking any other household object shows a private life which is difficult and full of frustrations and disappointments, mainly due to the fact that a close relationship is being harmed by major upheavals.

Carrying
Carrying news heralds the fact that a problem which has been troubling you for a long time is about to be solved, while carrying gifts is a warning to you to take care in business matters. Carrying a letter is a symbol of secrets which need to be kept. Carrying a heavy bag in a dream represents a burden you are bearing for someone else's sake. Carrying another person on your shoulders shows that you have a strong personality which others feel they can rely on.

Chaining up
Dreams about chaining other people up denote victory over foes, but being chained up yourself suggests other people are making life unduly difficult for you without your realizing it.

Cleaning
Dreaming about cleaning vegetables suggests petty argu-

Dreaming about dancing is usually a good sign

Driving a car in a dream symbolizes being in control of your life

ments within your family. Cleaning or washing clothes means excessive extravagance, while cleaning or polishing shoes means an aggressive exchange with a friend. Cleaning a house is a sign of joy and happiness, and cleaning a bath suggests your ideas are particularly well-thought-out and lucid at the moment. Cleaning a kitchen means that you are going through an optimistic phase and can expect good health; while cleaning or dusting furniture means you have inner vitality and great strength of will: both will stand you in good stead. Sweeping a path means that you can expect to be confronted by obstacles which are fairly difficult, but not by any means impossible, to overcome.

Copying

Dreaming about copying a letter is a sign of nervousness and anxiety, while copying a document indicates a strong, tenacious personality. Copying someone's signature shows you are involved in a difficult struggle with people who are much stronger than yourself, and unless you put your reason and practicality to work you could end up being humiliated. Copying someone else's behaviour in a dream, or following their instructions, suggests you have an unpredictable and extravagant personality and you should be careful to keep things in perspective.

Dancing

Dreaming about dancing with a partner is, in general, a good sign. If it is you dancing, there are gains and benefits on the way, while being at a ball indicates that a friend will enjoy a piece of good fortune. Dancing in a public place indicates a meeting which may change your life. It is only dancing on your own that brings sadness in real life: you have hopes which will never be realized.

Dancing a waltz or hearing waltz music in a dream means that a minor misunderstanding could cause much harm to a long-standing relationship, though fortunately it will not do any permanent damage.

Digging

Dreaming about digging a ditch means you need something new and different to happen in your life, while digging a hole symbolizes debts to be repaid as soon as possible. Digging a well indicates differences with members of your family. If you are involved in digging for some kind of precious metal or stones, you are subconsciously aware that there is hostility towards you at work.

Driving

If you dream of someone else doing the driving, then your dream has hopeful implications, but if you are driving a car or other vehicle, it may mean that you will lose, or spend unnecessarily, a large amount of money. Driving a car in a dream also symbolizes being in control of your own destiny; it may also mean differences of opinion with those dear to you. Driving a lorry indicates that you will shortly find a solution to a major problem which has been worrying you. Driving a tractor means that you are feeling very secure about your future, and riding a moped or motorbike is also a sign that you feel you are in control of your life and where you are going.

Flying
See *Sensations*

Freeing yourself
The meaning of this dream depends on what you free yourself from. Freeing yourself from people who are annoying you indicates a need for independence, while freeing yourself from a promise or obligation heralds a difficult time in which careful reflection is required. Freeing yourself from chains or escaping from prison shows that you have great energy, and ridding yourself of parasites indicates shortlived problems.

Giving or receiving a gift
Receiving a gift from someone you know in a dream is not a good omen, suggesting that in real life you should take a long, hard look at the giver of the gift in the dream to see if you can trust them. Being given a present from a stranger means a reconciliation with someone you love occurring in the very near future. Giving someone else a gift, on the other hand, is a sign of your great pleasure at an unexpected personal success. The act of buying a present in a dream symbolizes your discouragement and depression at an emotional upset which you had not expected.

Giving a useful present means you will be involved in a major setback, while if you give a decorative present you will have to take a very important decision shortly. If you give an expensive present, you will soon find yourself in a situation which is favourable to your plans and ambitions. Giving or receiving a gift of money in a dream signifies that a business matter must be sorted out. However, it may also signify the ingratitude of people around you. Receiving good wishes in a greetings card indicates harmony in emotional relationships. A gift of flowers shows that you have a sensitive mind.

Hiding
Hiding anything in a dream indicates you are shy and introverted and tend to give your partner too little space to develop within your relationship. More particularly, hiding money suggests nervous tension and susceptibility to the influence of others. If you hide from something you are afraid of, you have secrets which are not particularly well kept and prejudices which you need to overcome.

Interviewing
Interviewing an entertainer of any kind in a dream means there is a pleasant meeting coming up soon, while interviewing a politician denotes a rebellious personality. A job interview in a dream indicates a major change, not necessarily connected with your career, and any interview involving a woman indicates that you are highly-strung, possibly because an underlying problem is unresolved.

Lingering
To dream of lingering in conversation when you should be doing something else can have various meanings. If you are talking to men, the dream signifies a happy relationship, and if to women, you can expect at least one new friendship in the near future. If you are lingering in conversation with friends, it can indicate either recent heated, but friendly, discussion, or violent arguments. Lingering in conversation in a pub indicates a lack of loyalty to someone.

Opening something
Opening a door in a dream means you are receptive to new developments. Opening a lock suggests you will make a find or discovery in your own home. Opening a safe suggests you have no secrets from members of your family. If you open a tin, it suggests that something you have done recently will have unexpected repercussions; opening a box means you will be rewarded for your patience.

Painting
If you see an artist at work in a dream, it shows you will undergo a period of anxiety for no particular reason, while if it is a painter of the decorating variety, a much-needed compromise will be reached.

The significance of a painting in a dream varies according to the materials used and the subject of the painting. An oil painting suggests there are difficulties ahead, and a watercolour signifies pride. A still-life painting shows that you are admired by other people, and a landscape means you are at peace with yourself. A seascape is a sign of depression, and a portrait or figure painting indicates short-lived victories.

Parachuting
Making a parachute jump means you are feeling very self-confident and very much aware of your abilities, but if you see someone else making one, you should take care of yourself because your health may be at risk. An opened parachute denotes an inbred sense of optimism.

Dreaming of a parachute wrapped up in its bag means that you face a choice between two potential relationships: you should put a great deal of careful thought into which you choose, because it will be a deciding factor in the way things go in the future.

Passing
Dreaming of passing through a field indicates your susceptibility to unpredictable outbursts of anger. Passing someone you know in the street without recognizing or

greeting them means you are putting your own needs before other people; but if you do acknowledge them, you are likely to be a charitable and kind-hearted person. Passing a building without going inside indicates that you do not pry into matters which do not concern you and also that you can keep a secret. (Passing an examination means you are particularly worried about what the future holds in store for you.)

Materials and subject determine the dream's precise meaning

Patrolling
Patrolling the streets of a city in a dream, perhaps in a police car, means you are original and imaginative in your ideas. If it is daytime, you will be the object of the criticism and gossip of others, but if it is night, you are being over-romantic in your relations with your partner and unless you are more down-to-earth you will lose his or her love. Patrolling a forest means exciting events are on the way.

Raid
A raid by thieves or bandits in a dream shows a confused and uncertain emotional relationship: you need to sort things out in this area or you will lose the love and respect of the person you love. If you are raided by the police in your dream, you have some minor personal problems at the moment, but if you manage to avoid arrest, a piece of work you are involved in will end happily.

Reacting
Seeing a man reacting violently to something in a dream means you will find yourself caught up in a very delicate situation and have no idea how to get out of it; if a woman reacts violently in a dream, this indicates that you are a sensitive, slightly timid person.

Recruiting
To dream of being recruited into the armed forces indicates that you have had difficult times at work recently which have taught you something about yourself and helped you to become more independent. Being recruited into a team to play any kind of sport means you will have a major difference of opinion with relatives. Employing workers yourself means you are over-reacting to situations and being impulsive and jumpy: you should try to calm down and face up to the problems of everyday life with a little more reflection. Recruiting soldiers in a dream means that soon you will have a very favourable opportunity.

Renouncing
Renouncing a religion in a dream suggests that an important project at work will be brought to a speedy and successful conclusion. Renouncing a right shows that you are very scrupulous in your professional life and show considerable attention to detail.

Repairing
Repairing a car in a dream indicates that you are careful with your money, though you are far from mean: and a bicycle, that you are feeling nervy and sensitive. Repairing shoes, or having someone else repair them, presages a tranquil, peaceful life. Repairing damage that you have caused through carelessness in a dream means that you are not always the most tactful of people.

Sacrifice
Sacrificing an animal in a dream suggests a minor disagreement with someone you work with; sacrificing a son or daughter foretells a serious difference of opinion with the person you love, which could signal the end of your relationship if the matter is not resolved amicably.

Searching
Searching for someone male in a dream indicates that you will find an obstacle to the smooth running of your plans at work which it will take all your powers of practicality and intelligence to remove. Looking for someone female in a dream means that you will be the object of criticism at work, but if you defend yourself, you will be supported by your superiors. Searching for an escaped prisoner means you will have to be careful not to get embroiled in a difficult situation. Searching for an object means you are being over-ambitious with regard to the future.

Shaving
Shaving yourself is a sign of financial loss, or uncertainty in business matters; shaving someone else presages provocation, but you should not rise to the bait.

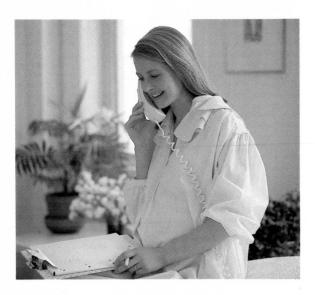

Your relationship may need first aid if you speak on the phone

Smoking
The exact interpretation of this dream depends on what is being smoked. Cigarettes mean you will have minor, insignificant financial gains, and cigars signify that your efforts are being made in vain. Smoking a pipe shows that you have received a just reward, and smoking drugs means you have a lot of important things to do. A cigarette holder reflects a delicate constitution and health.

Soiling
Soiled laundry in a dream indicates a distracted and worried frame of mind; wearing soiled clothes indicates your discouragement over something and your consequent mood of unhappiness. Soiled paper means that you have formed an unfair assessment of someone, and dirty furniture shows a lack of decisiveness and authority. If you dream about getting dirty in a pool of mud, you need to make a change in your work routine before your health is adversely affected by overwork.

Studying
Studying languages in a dream indicates that you are being deceitfully flattered and studying literature foretells of renewed hope in a project connected with your work. Studying maths means you have a habit of disagreeing with people for the sake of it. Studying in the evening means you are uncertain about what to do next in life.

Talking
Talking to a man in a dream indicates that new experiences connected with romance are on the way, and talking to a woman foretells advantageous business

dealings. Talking to an enemy indicates that arguments are going on in your family, and talking to an animal that significant financial losses or expenses are on the horizon. If you are talking loudly or shouting, you have a major obstacle to overcome, but if you talk quietly, or whisper, there will be malicious gossip about you. Speaking ill of someone indicates a recent outburst of bad temper, and speaking well of them indicates that you have some bad habits. Listening to someone else talking indicates that you are impulsive by nature.

Telephoning
Speaking to someone on the phone in your dream indicates that an apparently small difference of opinion with your partner could have a much more serious effect on your relationship than you might expect. If someone else phones you up in a dream, you have problems which will need to be sorted out within the next few days.

Throwing
Any kind of dream which involves throwing something indicates your present feelings of dissatisfaction. Throwing yourself into a river or the sea reflects a deep feeling of bitterness, and throwing yourself out of the window, a recent loss on the sports field. Throwing stones symbolizes your present mood of anger, and throwing a grenade suggests a temporary loss of self-confidence and self-esteem caused by a mistake.

Undressing
Undressing a child in a dream reflects your realization that you must stand up for your rights. Undressing a man indicates unfaithfulness in a relationship, and undressing a woman shows that you may be displaying a lack of scruples in real life. Undressing a body ready for burial means a dangerous situation is looming. If you undress indoors you will make an unusual acquaintance, and if you undress in the street you need to rest after an exhausting piece of work.

Urinating
Urinating on the ground during a dream suggests that you are facing annoying problems and obstacles, and urinating in the street means belated regret for something unpleasant you did in the past. If you dream about wetting your bed, financial gains are on the way, and a child wetting himself or herself means that you can expect a heated argument with your partner.

Walking
This dream has different interpretations, depending on where you are doing the walking. Walking along a mountain road or path indicates future success and health, but walking along a narrow lane in a town or village

foreshadows misfortune. Walking with difficulty on sand or snow denotes a feeling of insecurity, but walking on grass or in the countryside signifies your present state of calm and contentment.

Washing
Washing clothes in a dream indicates health and financial security, and washing crockery suggests family difficulties. Washing a floor indicates your experience of minor setbacks, and washing windows indicates that you have recently avoided a danger of some kind. Washing yourself indicates future joy and happiness, though washing your face foretells a short-lived sadness, and washing your hair shows there is a surprise in store.

Wrapping a parcel
Wrapping up goods in a shop in a dream means you are consolidating and strengthening your position at work, though if they are very large items, such as pieces of furniture, which are difficult to wrap up, the dream suggests that a friendship or relationship will end. Wrapping up a present means you are keeping your feelings about someone to yourself for the time being until you are sure they are reciprocated.

Washing your face in a dream signals temporary sadness

4
Nightmares and Fantasy

For thousands of years it was believed that evil spirits lurked in the land of sleep, waiting to possess the vulnerable sleeper. A nightmare, in fact, was thought to be one of these incubi, as they were called. Many old night-time prayers and psalms ask for God's protection during the hours of darkness, and it was common practise to hang a religious picture or crucifix over the bed as further insurance against evil.

Occultists say that nightmares represent real psychic attacks. Perhaps there is a malignant ghost haunting your home, or someone, somewhere is thinking harmful thoughts about you. Since telepathy has been scientifically proven to exist, the occultists could be right.

Nightmares can also be terrifyingly vivid re-runs of some deeply traumatic real-life event. Many soldiers have reported recurring nightmares in which they have re-lived the horrors of battle.

Strangely enough, but for a nightmare there might never have been a Second World War. In November 1917, the young Adolf Hitler was a corporal in the German army, fast asleep in his bunker, close to the battleground by the Somme. Dreaming that earth and debris were suffocating him, he woke up and ran outside. Moments later a French shell struck his bunker, killing everyone inside.

Fantasy falls into a separate category, and such dreams have often inspired poetry, music and art. Mary Shelley based her novel, *Frankenstein*, upon a strange and fantastical nightmare – while both John Bunyan's *Pilgrim's Progress* and Samuel Taylor Coleridge's poem *Kubla Khan* sprang from the world of dreams. Many artists and writers have made creative use of their dream-time, for this is when the mind is freed from the bonds of reality and imagination can run riot.

Nightmares

Abyss

Seeing an abyss or crevasse or, worse still, falling into one, is a sign of great danger which even your friends are unlikely to be able to help you out of. Take particular care in your life and keep your eyes open.

Blood

Human blood is a symbol of success in one's endeavours, while animal blood means that you need some of your responsibilities taken off your shoulders if you are to function efficiently. Dried blood is a symbol of a fairly major problem at work. Any dream in which you see blood suggests that you should keep contacts with a new acquaintance to the minimum for the time being.

Burning

Any kind of fire burning in a dream has a positive significance, though the exact meaning depends on what substance or object is burning. Burning wood indicates liveliness of mind and inventiveness, as does smoking tobacco; while burning incense or perfume of any kind stands for sympathy or warmth coming from a source you had not expected. Burning oil or petrol is sounding a note of caution to the dreamer, but a house burning signifies that relief is on the way from problems or an illness that has been distressing you.

A fire in a grate in a dream symbolizes energy and health. A large, warm fireplace in a room indicates good fortune, wealth and – for those in love – the realization of their desires. Putting a fire out, on the other hand, means there are problems for you in prospect – as does being burned by a fire. An artificial fire or an empty fireplace warns you of deceptive appearances in real life. A big, spreading fire, such as bush fire, tells you that events, and perhaps your own feelings, are getting out of control.

Lighting a flame in a dream indicates an adventurous frame of mind, but putting one out indicates competition and rivalry. A candle flame in a dream reveals indecisiveness with regard to a proposal, while a gas jet means a craving for freedom.

Calling out a name

If you dream about someone calling you by name, you are probably feeling highly-strung and irritable: you are going through a difficult time, and you need help and understanding to get you through it. Calling someone else by their name indicates a visit from someone you had totally lost contact with. Using a false name in a dream means you should be more careful because you have been making mistakes by not concentrating on the task in hand.

If you are in love, this scene is a good augury

Conspiracy

Taking part in a conspiracy in a dream shows that you are labouring under a major misapprehension or illusion. Discovering a conspiracy among others shows a piece of business being compromised to the point where it is no longer feasible.

A plot of any kind in a dream is a warning sign: keep yourself to yourself, and keep a close eye on friends and foes alike, because someone is scheming against you behind your back.

Corpse

This is a symbol of separation, parting, a break in a relationship or unfaithfulness in love. Dreaming about burying a corpse is a sign of good fortune at work. A dead body in a coffin is a sign of a bond being broken, while if you see one in a mortuary it indicates financial losses. The body of a woman reflects your being severely let down by a friend, while the body of a man means that you need to face up to those things in your life which are going wrong at the moment.

Crime

Any type of crime occurring in a dream is a sign of difficulties to come. A crime committed as a matter of honour or conscience is a sign that you have major worries, while a political crime suggests there are matters in your life which need clarification. Committing any type of crime yourself indicates that you are about to incur the displeasure of friends or colleagues.

Danger

If you feel you are in some kind of danger in your dream, without knowing exactly what it is, this shows you have a careful and prudent personality which will help you make major gains in a short space of time. If you come face-to-face with danger, you will go through a phase of being lazy and apathetic towards everything and you will not find it easy to free yourself from this state of mind. Even once you

Death in a dream is rarely an ill omen

achieve this, you may find yourself having difficulties with your partner.

Death

Death occurs quite often in dreams, and is rarely an ill omen: it simply shows that you are in a nervous or agitated state and being excessively pessimistic. Dreaming about your own death is a sign of both good health and improvements on the business or financial front, while it can also indicate meeting a person you have been attracted to for a long time on a more intimate footing than hitherto. Dreaming of being about to die indicates that your health may be at risk in a small way.

Similarly, seeing someone else dying in a dream indicates that you need to look after yourself and slow down if your health is not to suffer. If someone is dying and makes a will in a dream this indicates that there will be arguments and disagreements within your family. On the whole, the death of another person is a less favourable sign in a dream.

Devil

A dream in which the devil appears is, without exception, a sign of danger. Seeing the devil in a dream means there are major temptations to be avoided, and speaking to him means possible harm or damage has already been done. If you dream about being the devil yourself, a difficult time is on its way and you will have an uphill struggle to regain composure and tranquillity.

Disaster

Disasters in dreams can signify their opposite: good fortune and prosperity. If you are in love with someone, seeing or being a victim of a disaster in fact indicates that wedding bells will be ringing before long.

Drug

Dreaming about taking a drug of any kind, whether medicinal or narcotic, means you have too many illusions and fantasies and need to come down to earth. Dreaming that you are 'high' on a drug of any kind means that there is a potentially dangerous situation just around the corner. Buying drugs suggests you are putting money into something which will give you a poor return, but selling them indicates major financial gains.

Funerals

See *Life and Leisure*

Ghost

To see a ghost walking around in a dream indicates coming setbacks and financial worries, while a talking ghost signifies that you have dangerous illusions. If the ghost is wearing white you will enjoy good health, but if it is dressed in black, there will be bitterness and recriminations caused by your partner's unpredictable behaviour. If you don't run away from the ghost and it then goes away, you can expect good fortune in love and in business.

Gun or revolver
Firing a gun or revolver in a dream shows you are physically very fit and full of mental energy: this would be a very good time to start on a project of work you have wanted to be

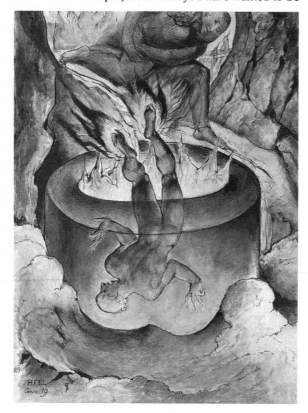

If you see hell in a dream, try and escape from it!

involved in for a long time. If you hear a gun being fired in your dream, you are full of brilliant ideas at the moment; if it is daytime in the dream when you hear it, you have financial problems which need sorting out before they start to snowball, but if it is night-time, you are in a nervous and restless frame of mind. If someone is shot in the dream, it means you have put an unpleasant phase of your life behind you for good.

Hanging
Tradition has it that if you dream about seeing yourself hanging from the gallows, it indicates a step upwards in the social scale. But seeing someone else being hanged

indicates a temporary or long-term lack of money.

If you also see a hangman in your dream, you are running a great risk in your emotional life. Climbing onto the platform of a scaffold means you have a reputation for being serious in your work and, if you are accompanied by a priest, it indicates that you will be plagued with feelings of fear and anxiety; fortunately, they will not last for long.

Hell
As you might expect, hell is an ill omen in dreams. If you dream about going there, or even of just seeing it, misfortunes, illness and monetary losses are in prospect. Escaping from hell, on the other hand, is a sign of good fortune in times to come.

Killing someone
If you dream about committing a homicide, you should avoid a temptation which would harm your reputation, no matter what the cost to yourself may be in terms of emotional turmoil. If you kill someone on purpose, you need to have another look at some of your opinions,

A kitchen knife in a dream warns of danger

because they may prove to be wrong. If the death is accidental, you are in excellent health and your worries about possible illness are unjustified. Planning a murder of any kind in a dream means you are intolerant and excessively talkative.

Killing your father, or someone else killing him, in a dream means you will have to make sacrifices, while your mother being killed indicates unpleasant remarks or actions from people close to you. Killing your lover means you may be involved in arguments with him or her which could ruin the relationship for good. If it is your husband who is killed in the dream, it indicates that you are a naive, impressionable person; while if it is your wife, it shows that you are harbouring unjustified suspicions and jealousy about her which you should take pains to clarify and correct in your mind.

Knife
An ordinary table knife is a favourable sign in a dream, indicating new conquests and successes. But any other dream involving a knife (a kitchen knife, or one covered in blood, or being sharpened), indicates possible danger and the need for great caution.

Mask
Just as masks are often used in real life to conceal the truth or hide faults and defects behind a superficial attractiveness or feigned sincerity, so in a dream they suggest that you or other people are being duplicitous and secretly jealous. Putting a mask on yourself in a dream means you need to look closely at your relationship with your partner to uncover the cause of present problems.

Monster
Not surprisingly, meeting any kind of monster in a dream is not a favourable indicator: it means you are going through a time when you are particularly depressed and pessimistic and this is making it difficult for the people you meet from day to day. Seeing a monster in the distance indicates emotional disagreements with someone, and being attacked or chased by one reflects your being disheartened by the failure of something you were involved in.

Night
Just as night has many unpleasant connotations in real life and in literature, so dreaming about the night indicates a period of crisis and indecision in a person who tends to be introverted and secretive. A really dark night means you are concealing your resentment towards someone who harmed you in the past, but a moonlit or starlit night symbolizes ambitions being fulfilled and the likelihood of an interesting discovery.

Nightmare
It is not at all unusual to dream about having a nightmare. It means you are being heavily influenced by someone else's strong personality, and this could possibly have a harmful effect on you. The fact that you are not very clear in your own mind about matters at the moment is making it easier for this person to dominate you.

Pain
See *Sensations*

Duplicity can lie behind a mask in a dream

Punishment
As in real life, punishment is not pleasant in dreams. In most cases, it has an unfavourable meaning: punishing children, for instance, suggests significant financial problems are looming, and also, if they are your own children, that you are being over-emotional about something. If the punishment in your dream is justified (for example, a criminal receiving a sentence), you have a strong sense of responsibility, but if it is not, you are not managing to make your presence felt at work and to make people feel you are an important part of the team.

Robbery
If your dream involves your organizing a robbery, it suggests an inner conflict or dilemma which could have a permanent and injurious effect on you if you do not solve it

as soon as possible. Committing a robbery yourself in a dream shows your lack of self-control in real life, and being robbed means you will have an illness or injury which, fortunately, will soon be cured. Watching a robbery and not doing anything to prevent it suggests that you are insecure and full of self doubts.

Shipwreck
A shipwreck – if you are involved in it – is a portent of things going badly. You can expect a number of upsets and difficulties following a break with someone close to you, all of which will cause you to become very depressed. It also suggests your health is not as good as it could be, probably because you have been working too hard. If you see a shipwreck from a safe distance, on the other hand, the prospects are brighter in the areas of work and health.

Snake
The snake is widely regarded as a symbol of ill-fortune in dreams. If you see one in a dream, it means either an enemy is trying to harm you financially, or a rival in love is trying to destroy your happiness. If you manage to kill the snake, you will be able to prevent this person from damaging you.

More specifically, like all biting or stinging animals, the adder is a symbol of evil. Dreaming about one symbolizes suffering in love: your partner will prove unfaithful and deceitful and may bring you into discredit with his or her wayward behaviour.

Spear
If you or someone else are carrying a spear in a dream, it is a warning of potential danger: you should be particularly careful. Being wounded by a spear, or wounding someone else, signifies your great dissatisfaction with something or someone. A broken spear indicates major problems.

Sword
A very old sword in a dream foreshadows a brief setback on the horizon, and one being drawn out of its scabbard reflects financial problems which need to be sorted out before they get any worse. A bloodstained sword shows that you are subject to fits of depression which could have a more harmful effect than you realize.

Trap
If you dream about falling into a trap, you need to clear up a difficult situation which you have created through your own unpredictable behaviour. If you try to make someone else fall into a trap, you will be the victim of injustice.

Tunnel
A dark tunnel in a dream indicates repentance from an action in the past, while if it is lit you tend not to trust people around you and are worried about the future. Going through a tunnel in a dream means that a period of happiness is in prospect, both with your family and at work.

Vendetta
Having a vendetta against someone in a dream means that in real life someone – though not necessarily the person dreamed about – does not feel as strongly about you as you do about them. If someone else has a vendetta against you and wants revenge, you can expect problems at work.

Villain
Meeting someone who is evil in your dream actually has a favourable significance: it means that there is a letter on the way from someone you have a deep affection for.

Violence
This is not a very favourable subject for a dream, as it indicates major difficulties in the way of progress at work. If you are violent yourself in the dream, your feelings about your partner are no longer what they used to be.

Vulture
Dreaming of a vulture has various meanings. If the vulture is flying, it indicates the harmful activities of enemies or rivals in love, but if it is devouring carrion, it suggests that fortune will smile on you and you will stop being plagued with worries. Killing a vulture is a good sign in a dream: it shows that you have finally overcome your misfortunes.

Dining vultures herald good fortune

Creatures of the night

Seeing a witch in a dream suggests a restless frame of mind

Jackal
Dreaming about a jackal is not an optimistic sign. The animal symbolizes an enemy waiting for a weak moment to attack, though if you move carefully, you can turn things against him.

Skeleton
A human skeleton in a dream indicates that serious financial worries lie ahead, and an animal's skeleton suggests that you have a tendency to feel lonely and depressed, though if you accepted the help of someone who cares about you, you could shake off this state of mind. If the skeleton walks or talks, it indicates that you have a secret which you would be very reluctant to confide to anyone.

Skull
A human skull suggests a sense of worry and lack of trust in someone close to you, and an animal's skull indicates that you are in some embarrassing situation. A talking skull symbolizes your well-kept secrets.

Vampire
Dreaming about a vampire means you are full of problems and fears. Being bitten by one indicates the chance of a future unpleasant encounter, but if the vampire gets killed in the dream it means there are better times ahead.

Witch
Seeing a hag or a witch in a dream brings ill luck and is a symptom of a highly-strung, restless frame of mind. Seeing one riding on a broomstick means there will be a scandal which will harm your image and put your job at risk; if the hag talks to you, your reputation is being impaired by someone you know.

An old witch in a dream suggests your ideas about a new project are misguided and unlikely to be feasible, and if she is also especially ugly, it means you are indulging in an empty flirtation which will not do you or the other person any good in the long term.

Wolf
A wolf is a distinctly bad omen if it appears in a dream. Hunting a wolf means there is danger on the horizon, and being chased by one means you are anxious and worried. Killing a wolf, on the other hand, means a success of some kind is imminent.

Fantasy and Spirituality

The Good and Bad
Fairies at the
Christening of the
Princess Beauty

A fairy in a dream is a bearer of good tidings

Angel
The appearance of an angel is an extremely favourable sign in a dream, as it indicates a major increase in other people's respect for you. If there are many angels and you are in their midst, you can look forward to a happy life with many friends you can trust and rely on.

Dream
Interestingly enough, it is quite common to dream about having a dream, and usually it indicates a period where things are going your way. If you dream about having a pleasant dream this suggests that new developments will happen at work.

Fairy or giant
A fairy is invariably a bearer of good tidings if it appears in a dream, indicating riches and good fortune.

A giant appearing in a dream is a sign of danger, but if you kill the giant or get the better of him in any way, you will be able to overcome the difficulties that presently lie in your path.

God
This is always a comforting, reassuring subject for a dream: seeing God indicates happiness; speaking to him, well-being; and praising him, a strong sense of moral responsibility. Praying to God in a dream is a sign that you have solved a problem.

Magic potion
Making a magic potion in a dream suggests that you should look out for cheating and deception going on around you, and drinking one indicates the arrival of interesting news from a long way away. If the potion is made from herbs, you will gain a great deal of money; if it is sweet, you need to be less selfish and make sacrifices if your relationship with your partner is to go the way you want it to; if it is bitter, you are making your presence felt in your work. A medicinal potion means you have a decisive and resolute personality. Making someone else drink a potion shows that you have made a recent error of judgement.

Paradise
This dream is naturally a pleasant augury for the future: going to paradise means you will be protected and supported by someone who has a great deal of influence, and being there suggests the possibility that a venture at work, which has previously failed, will now be tried again. Seeing your own father in heaven means you are careful and rational in everything you do, while dreaming that your mother is there means that there will be a sudden change within your family. Dreaming about an earthly paradise – perhaps a tropical palm-lined beach – indicates long-lasting and secure financial prosperity.

Treasure
Owning treasure in your dream means you are about to go on a long and successful business trip. If you find hidden treasure, you will not manage to complete a project at work which you had high hopes for.

Wish
If you make a wish in a dream and it comes true, it suggests you are a sympathetic, caring person and this will stand you in particularly good stead in a new relationship which is just starting to develop. If your wish does not come true, it suggests you have been taking too seriously criticism which, although well meant, is not justified.

Royal dreams

Side by side in a dream, a king and queen signify success

Castle
Usually this means arguments with others caused by your shortcomings, but a castle can also have other meanings. An ancient castle, possibly a medieval one, indicates that long-term investments need to be reviewed, while a castle being demolished or burnt down is a foreboding of danger. A castle under siege shows that you are involved in a quest for freedom.

Crown
Dreaming about a royal crown is a sign of social advancement, but if you dream about donning it yourself you may be rather uncommunicative and untrustworthy at the moment. A golden crown symbolizes responsibilities involving trust, and a crown of flowers, delicate health.

King or queen
A king seated on his throne in a dream suggests there is a danger of someone cheating you. A king being crowned is a symbol of business matters going well, and one holding a sceptre shows your increasing energy and strong force of will. A king standing beside his queen symbolizes initiatives you have taken being successful. If the king is a young man in your dream, you will be criticized and abused behind your back by a colleague at work who dislikes you, but if the king is old,

you will enjoy a major personal success.

A queen sitting on her throne in a dream denotes good fortune and success in business affairs. If you see her waving from a balcony, she heralds the arrival of news from distant parts, and if she is in a carriage, it shows that you may have a lust for power and fame which makes you look ridiculous. If she is side by side with the king, this shows that your enterprises will end in success. A queen bee in your dream means you will enjoy perfect health for some time, but a queen in cards means you are over confident.

Palace
A palace being built in a dream means a change of plan, while one being knocked down indicates tyrannical behaviour. If it falls down, a romantic liaison will end. A glass palace is a symbol of a burden to be borne.

Your social life will perk up if you dream of a crown

Royalty
Dreaming about a royal family heralds financial success in the future, while dreaming of a prince foretells a pleasant and interesting discovery. A royal palace in a dream shows that you have had an unexpected stroke of good fortune. If you dream about putting on a royal gown, unfaithfulness in a relationship is indicated, and if you carry a royal sceptre, you will be criticized behind your back by people who are envious of you.

Throne
Dreaming of a throne for a king or queen indicates a calm confidence which will help you deal with a potentially embarrassing situation, while the Pope's throne signifies a correct decision.

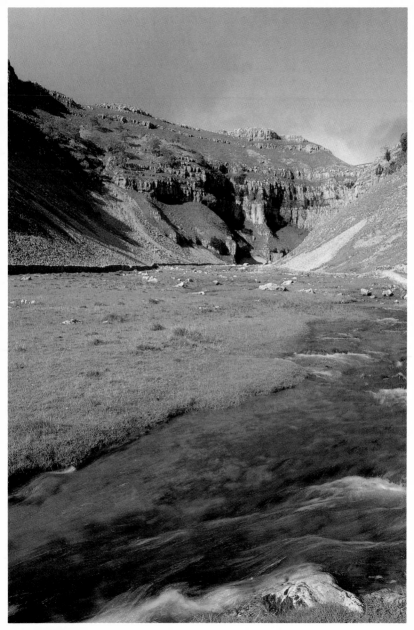

5
Nature

Numerous psychological party games are based on asking someone to draw or describe various natural scenes. Water invariably represents the life-force, or emotions – perhaps because we live in water as unborn children, and so it is the first natural element we know.

Nature dreams are often very enjoyable and almost always have a positive meaning. They suggest a well-balanced personality and bode well for future plans. Images of nature are, once again, very symbolic and may come from deep within the unconscious. Our environment may be a source of pleasure, boredom or destruction – and, however hard we try, we can never fully control it. In pagan times, nature was worshipped – with a different god or goddess for every part of the natural world.

Many of these ancient ideas still survive – although annual fertility ceremonies, such as dancing round the Maypole, have become almost meaningless. Others have been absorbed into Christian ritual, Harvest Festival being one of the most obvious examples. So nature dreams reflect our origins and our survival, and link us to the rhythms of life.

Our views of nature are often closely linked to our views of the outside world, and our place in it. If you dream of gardens filled with weeds and see storm clouds gathering, it does not take an expert to see that you must deal with a few problems in your waking life.

Typically, dreams of the environment are also full of subconscious plays on words and allegories. 'Earthy' people, someone who is 'a bit wet', to 'put down roots', and to 'breeze along' are just four figures of speech which may readily translate themselves into a dream landscape one night.

Nature

Air
If you dream about clear, clean air, this is a favourable sign; there is the chance to recoup some money you have spent or lost and also the chance of a pleasant journey to be made in the near future.

Avalanche
An avalanche signifies a high degree of impressionability and nervousness in the dreamer. If you are buried in the avalanche, you will be overwhelmed with sadness, and if the avalanche buries a house or hut or similar building, there will be discontent among your family.

Beach
An empty beach indicates a favourable opportunity which should be grasped as soon as possible. If there are people bathing, you have a great sense of security and confidence in yourself at the moment and an innate trust in the future. If you dream about sunbathing on a beach, business relationships will improve.

The sun behind clouds suggests a strong sense of duty

Clouds
If the sun is covered by clouds in your dream, you have a strong sense of duty and a careful, practical mind. If it is the moon that disappears behind the clouds, you are a patient and persevering person and these features of your personality will help you overcome the problems you are having at work at the moment. Any deterioration in the weather in your dreams reflects a change for the worse in your emotional stability: you are probably being unduly gloomy in your outlook. But a few white clouds are an indication of advancement in your working life.

Earth
Red earth in a dream reflects your own shyness and anxiety, while yellow earth is a symbol of false information. Black earth denotes gloom and depression. If you dream about picking up some earth, your physical strength is outstanding. Kissing the earth means that you will have disappointments in emotional matters.

Earthquake
A distant earthquake in a dream signifies a sudden, unexpected change, but if the earthquake is closer, this indicates that you will experience difficulties for quite a while. If the earthquake is prolonged, this suggests that you are worrying unnecessarily about a friend's health, but if the tremors are over quickly, this shows that you are nervous and irritable.

Eclipse
A solar eclipse indicates a shadow being cast over almost every aspect of your life. This will threaten the happiness of your relationship with your partner, your safety if you happen to be travelling anywhere, and also your future career. An eclipse of the moon, on the other hand, is a harbinger of good fortune, particularly if you are engaged to be married.

Evening
A moonlit evening in a dream symbolizes complications in love. A dark evening suggests your over-sensitive and childish behaviour will damage your relationship: if you do not change your ways you will lose the affection of the person you love. Passing a pleasant evening with one or more other people in a dream indicates that you can look forward to happier times.

Flowers
Different flowers have different connotations in dreams, though generally they foretell a period of happiness or good fortune which then – like flowers – withers and dies. Dried or dead flowers indicate obstacles and illnesses, but brightly-coloured, fresh flowers hold out better hopes for the future. A bouquet in a dream indicates an impending marriage. Arranging flowers reflects improvements in your life, and picking them and placing them in a vase suggests additional good fortune and the possibility of financial or other gains.

A garland of flowers in a dream promises either good news or shortlived pleasures. Having a garland on your head is a symbol of success attained in the face of slanderous remarks and petty jealousies.

A vase of flowers signifies financial gain

Fog
Just as in real life a fog casts a thick, silent mantle over everything and stops us seeing the things around us properly, so, in a dream, a fog shows that you have an introverted, mysterious personality which could cause problems in relations with those around you. If you dream of the kind of fog which is so thick that you can hardly see your hand in front of your face, there may be unseen dangers lying in wait, but if the fog lifts in your dream, you are being over careful. Getting lost in a fog in a dream suggests that the suspicions you have about somebody are unfounded and should be resolved.

Forest
Dreaming about going through a forest indicates a risky enterprise, but getting lost in one actually means that a project is guaranteed to be the success that you were hoping for.

Glade
A glade or clearing in the trees in a dream foreshadows a pleasant surprise. If there are flowers in the glade, there will be an unexpected journey to be made, while if it contains animals, good fortune and a strong will are indicated. If you dream about eating a picnic in a glade, there is a large amount of money coming your way, and if you go to sleep in one, you should keep a tight rein on your actions if you do not wish to damage a relationship irretrievably.

Grass
Grass is a pleasant omen in a dream, for it indicates prosperity and good health. Cutting the grass bodes less well, however, for it indicates that you are in danger of

It may be to your advantage to get lost in a forest!

being beset with financial problems in the near future, and grass which has gone yellow and dried up signifies that somebody's health could change for the worse.

Gulf
Dreaming of a gulf, either of water or empty space, symbolizes a sad parting from someone you love, though the parting might be avoided if you give them more care and attention.

Gust of wind
A gust of wind in a dream stands for the imminent arrival of unpleasant news and also indicates your fear of facing up to the future. Seeing something being blown away by a gust of wind means you are being domineering and possessive in your relationship with your partner and should avoid getting things out of proportion unless you want to lose love and respect.

If you are hit by hailstones you should cheer up shortly

about being at the top of a mountain, or a high hill, you will soon be rid of any hindrances standing in your way at work. Climbing a mountain indicates fatigue, and coming down from the summit of a mountain means you are being too timid and too melancholic, and both these traits could land you in trouble in your everyday life.

You could slip up if you dream about ice

Hail
Hail is not a promising subject to dream about, for it indicates an over-emotional state. Being hit by hailstones means your present state of melancholy is unlikely to last. In general, hail is a symbol of business losses, arguments between lovers, and bad harvests for farmers.

Harvest
Harvesting potatoes in a dream indicates that you are taking on a laborious, but profitable, task; picking apples or other fruit indicates a happy life in which most things are going your way. Harvesting grain means that you are now reaping the fruits of work you did a long time ago.

Hay
A haystack, or hayloft full of hay, indicates an unexpected stroke of good luck, but if the hay is wet, there are troubles in prospect for you.

Hill or mountain
A hill in a dream symbolizes a difficulty to be overcome. Dreaming you are standing on top of a hill means you have already put these difficulties behind you. If you dream

Hurricane
Tinea Ballater, the famous expert on dreams, says in one of her books, 'I wouldn't wish this dream on anybody.' In fact it is one of the worst things you can dream about, indicating that an extremely shaky period lies ahead in which, if you put a foot wrong, the result may be disastrous.

Ice or snow
Ice is not a good omen in a dream. If you see a vast expanse of snow and ice, or find yourself in the middle of one, it invariably signals either danger or difficulties of some kind. An icy road or path symbolizes restlessness and waiting for something new or interesting to happen.

Snow in a dream can have a number of different meanings. If it is light, powdery snow it indicates whimsical, capricious behaviour. Dirty slush reflects your discretion and carefulness, and a snowdrift indicates unexpected pleasures and financial gains. If snow is falling in your dream, there are many new and interesting events about to happen in your life, and if you are walking on snow, you have plenty of initiative and also considerable enthusiasm and imagination, but you should avoid getting things out of proportion which are troubling you at the moment.

Island
It is quite common to dream about being on a desert island, and this indicates your present boredom and loneliness. An inhabited island, on the other hand, indicates that interesting new developments are underway in some aspect of your life. A tropical island covered in palm trees foretells hopeful prospects, but if there is no vegetation on it, it means that things are going wrong because you have not treated them seriously enough.

Ivy
Ivy is a symbol in dreams of your assertiveness being put to good use, as well as of your faithfulness and tenacity. It promises total dedication in matters of love, loyalty in business affairs, and all-round success in life.

Lake
This dream can have both negative and positive aspects, depending on the context. It is an optimistic dream if you dream of a large, calm lake with clear waters, as it symbolizes future happiness and success. However, if the water is rough, or dirty, there is a difficult period in your life just ahead. Crossing a lake in a boat indicates that you have risen in the estimation of others; jumping into a lake suggests you are undergoing pain or unhappiness.

Success is on the way if you dream of a large, calm lake

Landscape
Most landscapes in dreams hold out the promise of happiness, and tranquillity in love. If you dream of a pleasant landscape, all your decisions are well-considered and promptly put into action. If the landscape is empty or unattractive, you will suffer a disappointment in matters of the heart which will leave a bitter after-taste. Dreaming of a seascape means you have a need for solitude, and a mountain landscape indicates that the past plays an important part in your life.

Landslide
Observing a landslide from a safe vantage point some distance away in a dream indicates that you are sensible and intelligent; but getting caught up in one indicates that there is cheating and deception between yourself and someone close to you.

Lane
Dreaming of a long country lane which stretches across the countryside indicates that a lengthy, burdensome task will soon be bringing its own reward. But if the lane is very narrow, it means that you must make some necessary concessions or compromises, while if the lane is blocked off, it means that you are troubled by personal dilemmas and doubts. If the lane is dark or in some way frightening, you have major financial problems at the moment.

Leaves
Like flowers, leaves in dreams bring good fortune, when they are green and healthy, signifying faithfulness in love, and harmonious family relationships. Fallen or dried-up leaves are a sign of difficulty and illness.

Lightning
Lightning momentarily turns night into day, and is therefore a healthy sign in dreams: seeing it flash indicates long-lasting good fortune. A tree, a house or anything else being struck by lightning means that you can look forward to the fulfilment of your plans in the future.

Marsh
If you dream about walking across marshland, there is a period of worry ahead and a difficult problem for you to tackle. If you get stuck in the mud, it means you will attract displeasure from others, but if you manage to get across to the other side without too much trouble, there are better times ahead. With regard to personal relationships, dreaming about a marsh indicates that you are about to enter a difficult period when everything on the emotional front seems fraught. However, this phase will pass and leave you much stronger.

Meadow
A meadow full of flowers in a dream indicates that your happiness and trust in your partner is being reciprocated by him or her. A newly-mown meadow indicates a worrying state of sadness and depression, and one with thick grass indicates illusions and vain hopes about the future. If you dream about walking through a field, you are set in your ways and most people would regard you as rather staid and conventional, while if you are sitting or lying in a meadow, there is pleasant news on the way. If you dream of going to sleep in a meadow you will soon experience a period of happiness.

Moon

Dreaming about the moon, which is a symbol of peace and harmony, is a very hopeful sign, particularly from the romantic point of view. The particular phase of the moon is also very important to the dream's interpretation. A crescent moon can indicate mental confusion and problems with your partner, though the latter should easily be overcome. A half moon indicates a hazardous journey, and if you see a full moon in a cloudless sky, a period of great happiness is in prospect, with the chance of a new relationship with someone of the opposite sex.

Oasis

A dream about an oasis is not always the favourable sign it might seem. Finding an oasis means you are being tetchy and irritable and need to calm down and relax for a while. However, drinking from a water source in an oasis indicates that you will overcome difficulties by hard work and concentration. Seeing an oasis in the distance means that you will undertake a new financial involvement or venture, but if you do not manage to reach the oasis, there will be minor family problems. If the oasis turns out to be a mirage, oddly enough, your hopes for the future will prove to be justified.

Ocean

Any vast expanse of water in a dream is a good omen, provided it is calm: it suggests an important project at work is about to be successfully concluded, and you will also make an acquaintance, or even a friend, who will one day be very useful to you. It also suggests things are going well in terms of romance, not least because your own likes and interests are so strongly reflected in those of your partner. If the ocean you see is a stormy one, there is exciting news on the way.

Panorama

A mountain panorama in a dream denotes inconsistency and restlessness, while viewing a panorama with a lake means that you have recently formed friendships that can be counted on. Stopping to admire a panoramic view, and perhaps taking photographs of it, means you are in superb health and are feeling zealous and enterprising.

Planet

Being an astronomer in a dream and looking at a planet through your telescope shows that projects you are involved in will develop slowly but successfully. If the planet is golden in colour, there will be a reconciliation with your partner after a difficult period caused by your obstinacy. If the planet is black, it shows you have made some ill-advised changes at work or elsewhere, but if it is any other colour it indicates your present feelings of peace and relaxation.

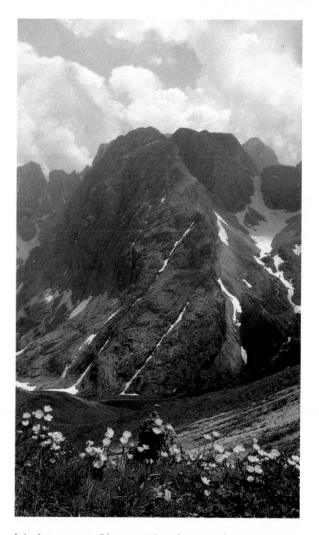

Itchy feet are a possible connotation of a mountain panorama

Plant

A flowering plant in a dream indicates unexpected happenings in the near future: if it is in a pot, there will be general changes for the better, but if it is growing in a garden or a field, you can expect interesting developments in relations with the opposite sex. A dried plant means you need to sort out an unpleasant misunderstanding, and a very small one means you have an aggressive, authoritarian personality which insists on its rights in whatever the circumstances.

Poppies

Like many other flowers in dreams, the poppy indicates happiness, though this happiness often does not last very long. Picking poppies in a dream foretells a short romance.

Rainbow

Even if you do not manage to find the traditional crock of gold at the end of it, dreaming of a rainbow is very much a sign of good luck: there is change on the horizon, all of it for the good.

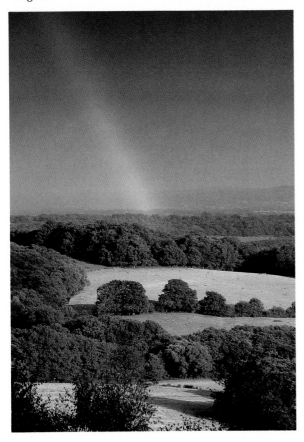

Good luck and a change for the better are brought by a rainbow

River

Dreaming of a river flowing along slowly and gently, or with clean water in it, signifies good fortune of some kind, but if it is rushing along, or if it is polluted or muddy, it indicates the opposite. Falling into a river in a dream means there is some kind of danger lying in wait for you; bathing in one indicates financial or material gains on the way; and swimming across a river foretells hopes coming to fruition.

Rock

Seeing a rock in a dream means that you have new opportunities for advancement at work, while moving one indicates your present gloom and dissatisfaction. Breaking a rock in a dream means that your emotions are empty and lifeless. Climbing up a rockface foretells your desires being

fulfilled, and getting off one indicates that you will launch a new venture with an uncertain future. If you fall off a rock in a dream, you will have to face up to the loss of a friend.

Shore

The shores of water are not generally an auspicious sign in a dream. Riverbanks represent your having impractical or dreamy ambitions, and a seashore shows inertia and laziness. The shores of a lake stand for sudden anger. If you land on an unknown shore in your dream, there is pleasant news on the way.

Snow

See *Ice*

Spring or stream

A spring with dirty water in a dream is an indicator of good fortune, but one which has dried up or blocked up indicates future problems and bitterness. A clear, clean spring is a guarantee of long-term good health, and drinking from a spring symbolizes the reciprocation of deep and lasting affection.

(A metal spring such as a bedspring suggests that you are not a materialistic person and can manage without your home comforts if necessary.)

If the season in your dream is obviously Spring, it symbolizes that you are having new and stimulating ideas.

Star

To dream of a star is a sign of confidence in yourself and your abilities; the pole star symbolizes hopes which are bound up with a project at work. If the star is twinkling, you should try to be more careful and cautious in things you do.

Storm

Any type of storm in a dream, be it rain, snow, hail or wind, is a sign that dangers are awaiting you and you need to be extra-cautious. A tempest at sea in a dream indicates that either your financial affairs or those of someone close to you need to be put into order, and a violent gale indicates harmful thoughts and ideas. If you dream about getting unexpectedly caught in a storm, there will be significant changes at work which will help you attain a greater degree of independence and confidence.

Summit

Dreaming about a mountain summit with no snow on it means a journey of yours will have to be put off till later, but one with snow on it means you have made an unfair assessment of someone or something. If there are animals on the summit, it indicates improving health, and if there are plants or trees, you will reach agreement with members of your family. If it is shrouded in mist, your feelings towards someone are about to be reciprocated.

Sun

If the sun is shining brightly in your dream, it indicates that you will get much pleasure from a relationship with someone you love, but if it is obscured by clouds or anything else, there are unexpected obstacles at work.

Sunset

A sunset is a favourable omen in a dream. Although you may be feeling confused and bewildered at the moment,

A sunset means help and understanding are on the way

the help and understanding you will receive from your partner will help you regain your self-confidence and your enthusiasm for life, so that eventually you will be achieving things you never thought possible.

Thunder

A thunderstorm indicates your thoughtlessness over something or someone, while thundering waves mean that others cannot understand your actions. A thundering waterfall signifies that you hold a prejudice of some kind.

Torrent

A swollen torrent in a dream is a sign of your making influential friendships, but a dried-up river bed shows a lack of practicality. A wide torrent indicates future tranquillity and prosperity, but a furiously raging one predicts the opposite. If your dream involves crossing a foaming torrent, it suggests you are cautious and careful in everything you do.

Tree

If you dream about a tree with plenty of foliage and bearing fruit, it indicates future financial prosperity, and a happy marriage blessed with children. If you climb the tree, not only will you achieve both these goals, but an even greater blessing – contentment. However, a tree being cut down means a loss of a friend or of money, and a tree being battered by a storm symbolizes major family problems.

A large oak tree in a dream is a sign of your strong willpower and decisiveness, but a stunted oak indicates that you may attract enmity and hostility in the future which could be dangerous, and one which has fallen over suggests that an argument with your partner is looming. If the oak has been uprooted, differences of opinion will arise within your family. A leafy oak indicates changes for the better in your work environment, but if it is leafless, you are likely to be surrounded by people who are working against your interests. Cutting down an oak shows flagging energy, and chopping one up shows your present lack of self-control. If you climb up an oak in your dream, you are being far too ambitious, while if you are stretched out beneath one, you can expect a period of excellent health and considerable prosperity.

The palm tree is a very auspicious symbol to dream of, indicating success, prosperity and happiness. It is also a favourable omen for anyone who is in love. A date palm means there is interesting news on the way, and a coconut palm means the situation between you and your partner will soon return to normal. An oasis of palm trees signifies new hope where romance is concerned.

Valley

Dreaming of a dark, sunless valley indicates a contented, tranquil existence. A very deep valley symbolizes a profitable venture, but if you dream of a valley with cultivated fields in it, you need to change your ways very quickly. If you dream about going into, or through, a valley, it means you are a lively, independently-minded person.

Vine

The appearance of a vine with black grapes on it in a dream shows you are enterprising; if it bears white grapes, your friendships are particularly strong. If you are growing or harvesting a vine in your dream, you have a trusting relationship with your partner, and if you are pruning it there will be an improvement in your finances.

Water

Dreaming of any expanse of rough water means there are problems in store, though if you cross it successfully you will overcome all the obstacles in your path. Drinking water is a bad sign, as it indicates poverty looming on the horizon, and bathing and swimming in dirty water indicates that some kind of danger is on the way. Falling into water means that a reconciliation is forthcoming.

Waterfall

A waterfall is a favourable omen in dreams. If it is exceptionally large, it reflects a sensible, reflective personality, and if it is only small, you are likely to be a patient, tolerant person. If the waterfall is noisy, you are likely to be very energetic. Even falling into a waterfall yourself is a good omen – it means a win on the sporting field.

Waves
Dreaming about waves on the sea symbolizes recent, short-lived friendships, while those on a lake suggest that you are an intolerant and uninspiring personality. If your dream involves battling against the waves, either swimming or in a boat, it means you are strong-willed and obstinate and this can either be an asset or a drawback in your relationships with other people. If you or someone else is knocked down by a wave, you need to clear up an unpleasant family misunderstanding as soon as possible.

Wind
A pleasant, light breeze in a dream indicates a healthy financial position, but a violent gale signifies that you are facing an extremely tricky situation where you should be very careful before acting. If the wind is blowing against you, it indicates family problems, but if you have to shelter from the force of the wind it means there is reassuring news on the way. A bitterly cold wind means you are involved in negotiations, the outcome of which is uncertain.

Winter
Any winter landscape in a dream is a highly favourable sign, for it symbolizes financial and material successes.

Gardens

Fountain
Clean water always indicates good fortune in a dream, and this is also true of a clean fountain. A fountain which is dirty or has dried up indicates bitterness and troubles, and one that is working suggests abundance and good health. Dreams which involve drinking from a fountain are a symbol of love being reciprocated.

Garden
A well-kept garden full of flowers in a dream signifies a good harvest for the farmer, advantageous deals for the businessman, happiness for lovers, and good news for people in general. But an abandoned, overgrown garden indicates a period of confusion and difficulty.

Cultivating a vegetable garden or allotment in a dream means that your business and financial affairs are about to take a dramatic turn for the better. Putting fertilizer on the garden indicates your renewed hopes on the romantic front; watering it, unexpected financial gains; sowing seeds in it, a practical and sociable nature. Any dream which involves your working in a vegetable garden suggests you can expect some good news, though digging up a garden with a spade suggests you are getting rich at the expense of others.

Maze
A maze in a dream is always a sign of problems, sometimes serious ones. Getting lost in a maze indicates uncertainty and indecision about which course to take in your life, while finding your way out of one means you have solved a major problem.

Park
A public park in a dream reflects satisfaction and fulfilment in relationships and at work, and a private

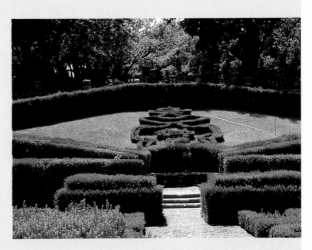

A private park indicates fast friendships are being formed

one indicates that you are making friendships that will never be broken. Going for a walk in a park on your own suggests you should set your sights a bit lower and not be so selfish, while if you walk with someone else, the current state of your affairs cannot continue for much longer – a radical overhaul is necessary. Getting lost in a park means that an error of judgement could compromise your position at work.

Roses
Growing roses shows that emotional relationships are going smoothly, and picking them symbolizes a new involvement, either in romance or business. Watering roses signifies support received from friends; giving them to someone, a great deal of personal prestige following on from a success; while being given them signifies receiving and giving love.

6
Money, Life and Leisure

There is an old saying that dreams go by opposites. Many of the traditional meanings of money dreams fall into this category – so that if you dream of great wealth, you are likely to be poor, or about to become so. This idea may seem implausible, but there is a valid explanation.

The conscious mind frequently compares and contrasts things. These mental comparisons help everyone to create an exact description of a person, place or situation. Most of us know that love and hate appear to be opposites although they are two very different faces of the same forceful emotion. Some schools of psychoanalysis argue that when we actively dislike someone or something, it is in fact a part of ourselves which we are afraid of.

When the subsconscious mind takes over, a process called the unification of opposites can occur, where the dreamer is unable to compare and contrast things – and so payment means loss, small means large and so on. It is like being a character in one of Lewis Carroll's *Alice* books. Some dreams about games fall into this surreal, upside-down world, while others can be more literally interpreted.

Dreams about daily life are relatively common, and often represent a mental effort to help the dreamer deal with what has been happening during the day. At other times they can be startling premonitions of real future events.

In 1968, the *Daily Mirror* published the true story of a predictive dream which was sadly ignored. A fifteen-year-old girl living opposite a block of flats, called Ronan Point, had a vivid dream in which the flats collapsed and people were running away from them screaming. She told one or two people who lived there, her friends and her mother. A short while later a gas explosion ripped the building apart, and part of it did indeed collapse.

Money

Bankruptcy
This is a warning signal to the dreamer. Dreaming about being bankrupt suggests that you need to be extremely cautious in business matters: it is better to follow the advice of others at the moment.

Coins
Dreaming about having coins in your pocket signifies good fortune, though not necessarily financial. You are likely to be making rapid progress in your job because of your extrovert, imaginative personality, but you have to be careful not to exaggerate things. Giving coins to a beggar means you can expect a prosperous period financially, while someone else giving you a coin or coins means you are about to experience a loss which will make you excessively cautious and pessimistic.

Debt
Owing someone else, or being owed money, is a sign of a certain amount of nervous tension on your part. Repaying a debt indicates confidence in your financial situation.

Financier
Dreaming about a financier or banker indicates an important meeting or appointment. If the financier lends you money, it indicates you are serious in your ambitions.

Handbag
If you dream about finding a handbag with money in it, you can expect good luck, in love if not in business matters. If it is empty, it suggests that you dislike routine and prefer it if something new and interesting is happening all the time. Losing a handbag indicates indecisiveness, and buying one, being extremely busy.

Inheritance
Inheriting something from a relative in a dream indicates the fact that you are worried about someone else's health, while if someone else inherits something, you may well lose a sizeable amount of money soon. If you dream about dividing an inheritance with other relatives, you are being much more emotional and highly-strung than usual: but if you keep calm, many of your problems will solve themselves. Losing or squandering an inheritance means that you are apprehensive about an important event.

Legacy
As you might expect, this dream has an entirely favourable significance. It suggests a pleasant surprise, possibly a gift of money, a visit, or a wedding.

Miser
Dreaming either that you see a miser, or that you are one yourself, indicates that you have to confront a wide variety of problems: your financial future is shaky, you will become involved in minor affairs without your partner's knowledge, and your ambitions will not be successful.

Money
Provided it is not present in excess, money in your dreams is always a harbinger of good luck. If you dream about giving away money, it shows that you can expect a period

If the coins are in your pocket, you will be in luck

of financial stability and prosperity, while if someone gives you some money in a dream there will be a major new development such as the birth of a baby or a significant success at work. Finding money is a very common theme in dreams, and it indicates a change for the better in your work or in your relationship with your partner.

Payment to make
Dreaming that you have a payment due, which you have not yet made, shows in fact that you are a responsible, thoughtful person and that you take your commitments seriously. Paying for something you have not bought means you need to change your tactics if you are to achieve your aims, while someone else paying you means that you will face obstacles and delays.

Saving money
The meaning of this dream depends very much on what is

being saved. If it is money, in the form of coins, the dream means that there are financial worries coming which will make life a great deal more difficult.

Selling

Selling something on credit in a dream means you are uncertain and unconfident. Selling something retail suggests you have a major burden or responsibility, and selling wholesale indicates a morbid imagination. Selling something by auction suggests your emotions need controlling. Selling things cheaply means work problems.

Signing a cheque or agreement

Signing a cheque in a dream signals difficulties in prospect, and signing a receipt indicates a recent outburst of anger

Selling in a dream suggests you are feeling burdened

on your part. Signing a letter indicates financial prosperity, and signing an agreement foretells career progress.

Subscription

If you dream about paying a subscription to something, the outlook is a very favourable one. It means either that you will soon obtain the vital results you have been waiting for for a long time, or that a secret will be revealed, or that your inquisitiveness about something will finally be justified.

Wallet

A leather wallet in a dream suggests you have had second thoughts about something, but it is now too late to make any changes. If the wallet has money in it, you have serious problems to overcome, though if you adopt a sensible, rational approach you should have little trouble dealing with them. If you dream about finding a wallet, an unexpected meeting is likely but losing one means you must now remedy one of your main faults, namely your uncertainty and indecisiveness. An empty wallet means there is money on the way, possibly from an inheritance or gambling win.

Wealth

More often than not, dreaming about being very wealthy means you are going through a prolonged period of gloom and self-doubt caused by your partner or by someone who loves you. If you try not to get too upset, but instead talk things through, the situation will eventually sort itself out.

Will

Making a will in a dream means you are about to get involved in a delicate situation which will need a great deal of diplomacy if things are to draw to a satisfactory conclusion. Reading a will suggests you should accept the help of someone more experienced than yourself.

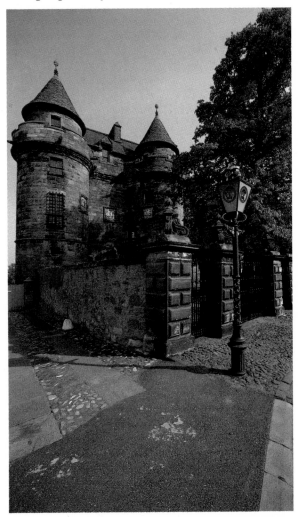

An inheritance may mean you are worried about someone's health

Career

It may not be plain sailing even if your work reputation is good

Employer
The appearance of an employer with whom you have good relations in a dream means that you will be shortly embarrassed by an unexpected piece of news. If you see your own employer in a dream, it means you are too emotional and impressionable. If you are summoned to your employer's office, there is an excellent chance of success in a new project you have embarked on. An angry employer in a dream shows that you have misplaced confidence in someone.

Pay
Receiving a weekly wage in a dream reflects a decision taken in too much of a hurry, while if it is fortnightly, you may be showing excessive wastefulness or extravagance. Being paid monthly is a sign of laziness. If you dream about being paid in advance, before you have done the work, it means that one false move at the moment could cause you a serious loss, possibly of money. Having your pay docked indicates, paradoxically, a feeling of personal and financial security.

Pension
Being paid a pension, or going to the post office to cash it, both mean there are problems in the offing involving your family. (If the pension you dream about is the guest-house variety, it means you are worried by how gloomy and despondent you are feeling, and you

should be careful not to get even more wrapped up in your problems, because then things will start getting greatly out of proportion.)

Publishing
To dream of having your books published shows that you are bored and depressed with your work, while being published in newspapers or magazines indicates that there is unpleasant gossip about you from people who are envious of your success. If you dream you are a reporter publishing an exclusive interview, you are likely to make great leaps forward in your work. Writing a review means you will feel less happy than usual in the future, but for no particular reason.

References
Showing someone your references in a dream means a financial venture you are involved in will be very successful; asking someone to provide them means you are far too egocentric and this is making you very difficult to live with. If the references are good ones, you are feeling very attached to someone you have met recently, but if they are bad, surprisingly enough, you will make undreamed-of progress in your career.

Reputation
Losing your reputation at work or at home is not a pleasant dream to have. It denotes jealousy and suspicion involving you and your partner. But even if you dream about having a good reputation for something, you could have a major conflict of opinion with someone you work with. If the reputation you have in a dream is bad, you are likely to be feeling ill at ease about something.

Resignation
Resigning from a job in your dream suggests that a period of major change is on the way. If you resign yourself in the dream cheerfully and gracefully to a job you are doing, it suggests you are an open, sociable person who reacts spontaneously to people around you, and even if you resign yourself to the task reluctantly, this indicates that you have a surprisingly intuitive and reflective personality. (Resigning yourself to having lost something means you are emotionally very sensitive, and resigning yourself to defeat indicates that your first impressions of someone you have just met are wrong.)

Life and Leisure

Baptism

Many dreams which involve going into a church are an ill omen, but attending a baptism is quite the opposite: it is a symbol of new life and happiness, though also a caution against complacency when one is happy.

Birth

Dreaming about a birth is generally a good omen, as bringing a son or daughter into the world indicates both a firm, decisive personality and financial and physical well-being. If the birth is a difficult one, there are major problems to be overcome and decisions to be made, though these will be resolved in your favour because you have a practical, rational mind. If the birth is an easy one, this reveals that you have considerable resistance to pain and suffering.

Celebrations

A birthday celebration signifies the beginning of an untroubled period in your life, while celebrating a festival such as Christmas shows you have a complex personality. Dreaming that it is Christmas is almost always a harbinger of good fortune, suggesting a favourable time for friendships, especially new ones, and a happy and fulfilling relationship with the person you love. Your health will be at its best. If you dream about Christmas Eve, though, this indicates a period of waiting, being kept in suspense, though eventually an advantageous piece of news will arrive and make you believe the waiting was worthwhile. Dreams which involve celebrating an unexpected event herald a period of stability and good health.

Circus

Although it might seem strange at first, a dream about a circus emphasizes the fact that things are temporary and short-lived, that happiness may be replaced by sadness, that projects and ideals may not come to fruition, and that friendships may place you at risk.

Competitions and winning

Dreaming about taking part in a competition, whether on the sporting field or elsewhere, indicates putting a disproportionate amount of effort into obtaining a result which does not justify the work involved; it also suggests a need to make use of all the reserves of tact and diplomacy you have at your disposal.

Winning a bet in a dream is a sign of shyness and timidity, while winning a competition or game suggests an imminent journey. Winning an argument or debate indicates good, co-operative relationships with people at work. Winning a game of chess means you are very much aware of your responsibilities and take decisions carefully and with forethought.

Concert

Going to a concert symbolizes an independent, entrepre-

The transitory nature of life is emphasized in this dream

neurial personality. Taking part in one shows that you are stubborn and obstinate, either in your current business relationships or generally, as a person. Conducting a band or orchestra in concert suggests you will be in the public eye in some way, but that your fame will be short-lived.

Examination

Revising for an examination in a dream suggests that you are a well-balanced, conscientious person. Undergoing a written exam indicates difficulties in your everyday life, while taking an oral one shows that you are proud of yourself and ambitious. Passing an examination in a dream shows that you have self-control and discipline; failing an exam, or not being able to answer any of the questions, indicates that you need to think more carefully before you rush into things.

Excursion

The meaning of this dream depends on the type of excursion and the mode of transport used. A trip into the countryside in a dream signifies that you will make a certain gain or profit, while a seaside excursion means that you will come into an unexpected income. An excursion into the mountains indicates that you will be travelling in the near future. A railway excursion suggests that your desires are being realized. An excursion on a boat means that you will soon have an unexpected visit, while travelling by bicycle suggests that you are spending too much.

Festival

Taking part in a festival, such as a street carnival, in a dream suggests that you are going through a stage of dissatisfaction and impatience. Any religious festival such as Christmas or Easter indicates that you have a spiritual side to your nature which is not being expressed.

Funeral

Like death, a funeral in a dream indicates the very opposite of what it seems to. It actually signifies health, and a marriage in the offing (not necessarily yours). Although the colour black often has negative connotations in dreams, it does not signify anything ominous or unpleasant when seen in this context.

Gathering

A reunion of former classmates in a dream is a sign of pleasant encounters, while a car rally indicates a slow and difficult ascent of the career ladder. Any other gathering of people in dreams means there are trials and tribulations to be overcome. If you attend a gathering at a friend's house in the dream, there is a period of happiness on the way, while a gathering of children shows interesting news in prospect. Gathering objects together means you will be used and then abandoned by the person you love.

Going out

Going out of a house in a dream symbolizes separation from someone you love; going out of a church means something you are involved in coming to an end, and going out of a hospital, slow, but inexorable, progress in your career. Leaving a theatre means you will suffer an emotional crisis in the near future but will emerge stronger for the experience.

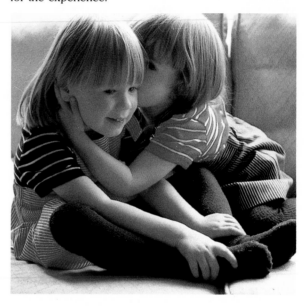

Your talents need to be realized at work if you reunite children

Meeting

Holding a meeting in a dream indicates that you are discontented and dissatisfied because of a lost opportunity, while taking part in one means you have a strong sense of responsibility and are decisive in everything you do. If the meeting is a particularly noisy one, there is a period of contentment on the way which others will be envious of.

Moving house

Most dreams which involve someone moving house are favourable ones; your present anxiety and nervousness will disappear and be replaced by an enviable state of contentment and calm.

News

Waiting for news about something in a dream suggests that you need to change direction in some of the things you are involved in at the moment because they are not giving you the results you hoped for. Being given news in a dream indicates satisfaction in your job. If you receive unpleasant news, you can expect to have to postpone a trip abroad because of problems you had not anticipated. If it is pleasant news, try not to get involved in any uncertain or risky ventures, because they will not work out. Worrying news reflects hostility on the part of people you work with.

Reception
Holding a reception in a dream foretells advantageous business ventures and financial well-being. Going to a reception indicates the beginning of new and exciting developments related to romance. If it is a noisy, informal reception, you are reserved and shy in almost everything you do; if it is a solemn, formal one, you are an original, imaginative person who loves anything that is risky or unusual. A reception held in your honour in a dream indicates that something is happening in your life that you are not accustomed to.

Reunion
Reuniting people in a dream is a sign that fortune is smiling on you and business matters are taking a turn for the better. Reuniting children suggests you have great talents which are still not being put to good use in your career, and a reunion of soldiers indicates heated and possibly hostile discussions with your partner. Reuniting school friends indicates the arrival of a major piece of good news, and reuniting relatives who have not seen each other for a long time means you are soon to embark on an emotional relationship which may not last.

A dream departure on a train suggests bright prospects

Setting off or departure
Setting off on a journey in a dream means a desire to escape and a craving for new experiences. Setting off on the right road means you have serious doubts about something, but setting off on the wrong one suggests that you will be successful.

Friends departing in a dream in fact signify possible visits by old acquaintances; relatives departing mean temporary setbacks; and a husband or wife departing means things between you and your partner are being

A visit to a relative indicates your vim and vigour

straightened out gradually and permanently. Dreaming about deciding on a departure date for a journey indicates that you have ambitions and ideas which are too lofty. If an actual dream departure is on a train, there are very bright prospects for the future; if by a plane, legitimate hopes and aspirations for the future; and departing by car means new burdens and responsibilities to be taken on if you are not to become too dependent on others in your work. If you depart somewhere by yourself, you will soon receive an interesting suggestion; while if you go with a friend or loved one, you will resolve your present financial difficulties.

Visit
Dreaming of a lengthy visit to a person or place indicates that a difference of opinion is being ironed out, and a short visit suggests that you should put off making a decision for the time being. If someone pays you an unexpected visit, on the other hand, it means you have an urgent problem to be sorted out. A visit to a relative means you have strong organizational skills and a great deal of energy, and one to a friend or acquaintance indicates that you need to be patient in waiting for the career advancement that you undoubtedly deserve.

Sport and games

If your dream boat uses sail power the future is rosy

Boat race
Watching a regatta, or any kind of boat race, is very common in dreams. It means there is news on its way, possibly from a great distance, which will give you hope and confidence in your future career. If you dream about actually taking part in a regatta, you need to make a temporary change of plans; if you win the race, there are difficult family arguments in the offing.

Cricket
Cricket is a game with complex rules, and seeing or taking part in a cricket match in your dream suggests you feel yourself bound by rules imposed on you by other people, but now is an opportunity to escape some of them. A cricket ball is a symbol of impatience which needs to be kept under control, and a cricket bat indicates petty jealousies and rivalries.

Cycling
Dreaming about a cyclist toiling up a hill, flying down it, or heading for the finishing post in a race indicates progress, triumphs over problems and adversaries, and other favourable changes. The only cycle dream which does not augur well for the future is that in which a cyclist falls off his bicycle – unless he or she gets back on and carries on riding!

Game
Playing in a game of any kind in a dream indicates heated, possibly violent arguments with your partner. Winning a game means that hopes connected with your profession are not being realized, and losing a game means you are getting the upper hand over your enemies. Selling games in a shop in a dream suggests you are deluding yourself that someone loves you when

they do not: don't run away with your illusions or you will make yourself very unhappy. A game which you win by a wide margin indicates differences with older people, and a friendly game indicates unstable relationships with the opposite sex.

Hunting
The meaning of this dream depends on what it is that is being hunted. Hunting a hare is a symbol of worries and troubles ahead, while a fox-hunt means lack of trust from someone close to you. Hunting a deer or a game-bird denotes intrigues involving someone you are in love with. If you are the one being hunted in the dream, it means that you are worried either by your responsibilities or by some problem that you are reluctant to face.

Lottery
Dreaming that you are taking part in a lottery is a bad omen from the romantic point of view. It indicates risks and uncertainty about the future, or, more precisely, it can mean that the behaviour of your partner is worrying you a great deal, and making you feel extremely unhappy and unsettled.

Puzzle
Solving a puzzle in a dream means you have finally taken control of a complicated situation in real life. An easy puzzle means that there are wrongs in your life which need righting, but if the puzzle is very difficult, your worries are fruitless and will go away much sooner than you thought.

Rowing
Rowing a boat strongly and effortlessly in a dream means you are too impulsive, and need to curb this side of your behaviour at any cost; rowing with tiredness shows your success in business matters; and rowing upstream shows your confusion of ideas and arguments with a superior at work. Rowing on the sea means you will receive support and protection from others at work, while rowing on a river suggests you are very much aware of your considerable abilities and are prepared to exploit them to the full. Rowing on a lake indicates that you are feeling highly-strung and irritable.

Sailing
Sailing across the sea in a boat in a dream suggests that you are an open, sociable person who also has considerable initiative, and this might be the time to put those qualities to good use by starting on a project you have been planning for some time. Sailing in a yacht

which uses sail power shows you have confidence in the future and in your own talents, but if your boat uses a motor, you have a strong mind and an awareness of your responsibilities, and there is also a letter on the way which may induce you to make a trip abroad to a particularly fascinating place.

Snooker
Seeing or playing a game of snooker, billiards or pool in a dream foreshadows possible difficulties on the horizon; if you are in love with someone, your family may be opposed to him or her.

Playing tennis means your drive for independence is strong

Tennis
Dreaming about a tennis court indicates a considerable sense of responsibility and rationality in your actions, while if you see someone else playing tennis, rapid advancement in your career is just around the corner. Playing it yourself means you have a strong need for freedom and independence.

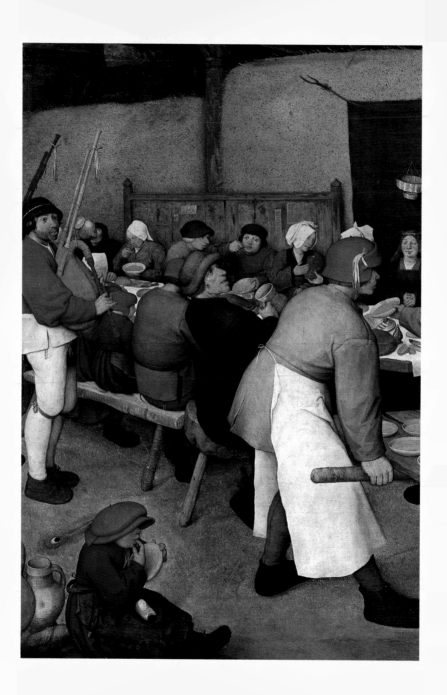

7
People

People of every kind figure in dreams, providing a rich stock of images and possible interpretations. Freud's pupil, Carl Gustav Jung (1875–1961), paid great attention to the sometimes extraordinary figures which people our dreams. He believed them to represent parts of the dreamer's unconscious or, alternatively, archetypal figures.

Jung's idea of the archetype is a fascinating one. He believed that everyone can tap in to a kind of universal memory bank, or collective mind, which forms a source of images that are common throughout mythology, fairy-tales and folklore. These images are often presented in the form of people such as the wise old woman, the beautiful princess, the brave knight, and the evil villain. Such figures are symbols, just like the gods of old, and represent an underlying emotion or principle.

When you dream about someone, it can be interesting to ask yourself exactly what he or she represents. Perhaps he or she has qualities you are trying to develop, or stands for a neglected part of your personality which is trying to make itself felt. Some dreams of the opposite sex fall into this category, for we all contain elements of both male and female within us, whatever our physical gender.

Dreams of other people can be predictive, or tell us something about the person that our conscious mind may not have noticed. Telepathy, too, has played a part in many dreams during which we are actually tuning in to someone else's thoughts and feelings while we sleep.

Mothers have dreamed accurately about their unborn children; family members or close friends have dreamed of the death of those close to them, only to find their dream has come true within days; and numerous people have dreamed of distant friends shortly before hearing from them. Always pay close attention to your dream visitors, for they are bringing important and enlightening messages.

People

Athlete
An athlete or sportsman in a dream is not a sign of good luck; you could be entering quite a difficult phase of your life in many respects. You may experience a break with someone you love and with whom you have been building up a relationship for some time. In work you are likely to make a series of mistakes which will lose you the respect of one of your superiors, and ill health is also indicated. If you dream about being an athlete yourself, you will experience a disappointment in love.

Baby
This is a very auspicious dream to have, as it symbolizes happiness and success in everything you do. But if a girl dreams about babies, it is possible that someone is trying to seduce her.

Dreaming of an explorer reveals a fear of the future

In most cases, a dream about a newborn baby is not a healthy sign; it suggests a strong, almost childlike dependence on your part or that of someone close to you. It also indicates that you are exhausted because of the repeated failure of something you are involved in at work, leading to a general feeling of hopelessness. If the baby is crying, it means you can take courage because you will be helped by advice given by someone very close to you.

Beggar
Despite what it might seem to imply, seeing a beggar in a dream shows that a period of happiness and lack of worry is just around the corner. Most importantly, financial matters are likely to go well, while in love you will meet the person you were looking for and they will give you happiness. But if you dream about being a beggar, you are the object of hostility though this will not harm you.

Bishop
A bishop seen in a church is a sign of new developments in an old situation. If he is standing at the altar, the outlook for the future is highly optimistic, and if he is in a procession, serenity is indicated. If the bishop is giving communion, there will be a happy event within your family.

Boxer
A boxer in the ring signifies that you are having difficulty in choosing from a variety of options open to you, while if he is on the ropes, you have been brought down to earth after a period in which you were suffering from illusions. If the boxer wins the match, you can expect exciting new events to occur soon, but if he is knocked out you may lose something which is precious to you. A black boxer symbolizes wasted energies, while a white one shows up conflicts and friction with relations and friends.

Boy
Dreaming about a schoolboy indicates breadth of vision and generosity. A boy in church, possibly an altar boy, means you are being too impulsive and flighty. If you see boys eating in a dream, your feelings towards your partner are genuine, but if the boys are arguing or fighting, you lack understanding and affection for your partner.

Explorer
Dreaming about an explorer on his travels suggests that you fear what the future might hold. An explorer who is lost or injured in a dream means you are worried about something. If you are doing the exploring, it shows you are imaginative and have a spirit of adventure.

Face

Dreaming about seeing your own face in a mirror means that a secret project in which you are involved is about to come out into the open. If you see a happy, smiling face, it indicates happiness in your daily life, and, conversely, if the face is sad, you will be sad yourself. The face of someone you know in a dream indicates an invitation to a celebration, while one you do not recognize means there are upheavals in prospect. A man's face in a dream shows that you have confidence in the future, but a woman's face signifies that you are beset by doubts about the future.

Girl

The appearance of a beautiful girl in a dream signifies romantic fulfilment, while an ugly one means you are spoilt for choice in some area of your life. A laughing girl in a dream symbolizes unexpected expense, and a crying one, major financial problems. If the girl is asleep, you will meet with an unanticipated obstacle in your work; if she is studying, you have bright prospects for the future. If the girl is ill, there will be new romantic conquests, and if she is dead, you will be let down by someone close to you.

Grocer

Going into a grocer's shop in a dream means that your actions or initiatives have a good chance of success. Being a grocer yourself reflects annoyance and disagreements within the family, and buying groceries means a calm state of mind. If the grocer's is closed, it means you can expect a project you were involved in to come out right in the end.

Guard

A night-watchman in a dream signifies the possibility of a theft or other crime, while a military guard at the gates of a barracks or elsewhere means that you are being illogical in your behaviour at the moment. Being on guard yourself indicates an imminent loss of money.

Hunchback

Tradition has it that meeting a hunchback in a dream will bring pleasant news not long afterwards, and if you manage to touch the hunchback you can expect good luck and personal success. Being a hunchback yourself, though, suggests your health is not as good as it might be.

Jesus

If you have the good fortune to dream about Jesus, there is a long period of physical and spiritual well-being in prospect. If you talk to him, or he talks to you, this indicates that you are full of hope for the future.

Jury

If you see a jury in your dream, it is a promising sign, but this is not the case if you are part of the jury yourself.

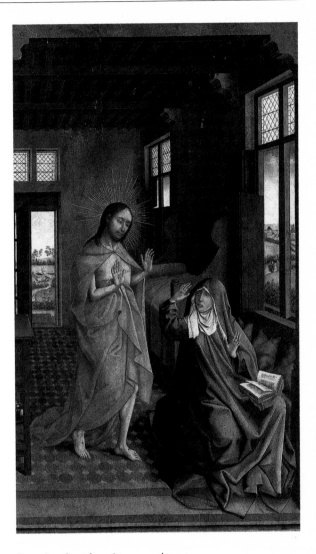

Dreaming about Jesus is very good news

Labourer

Seeing a man involved in any kind of heavy work in a dream, such as pushing a wheelbarrow or unloading things from a lorry, has pleasant connotations: a fortunate coincidence is on the way that will bring you both money and respect. If the labourer is having a rest, your working life is stagnating because you are lacking in willpower and enthusiasm.

Any kind of worker in a dream suggests that the effort you are putting into something important will be rewarded with success. Dreaming of a manual worker at work means that there are ambitious projects in store for the future. Dreaming about a clerical or managerial worker suggests that you are at a difficult stage in your career. If you employ workers of any kind in your dream, it suggests that your career prospects are very bright indeed, but if someone close employs you, it may be that someone in life is taking advantage of your good nature and friendly disposition.

Madman or madwoman
Dreaming of mad people in a hospital or asylum indicates that you have recently undergone some unjustified humiliation, while mad people in the street suggest hostile gossip going on behind your back. If the mad are confined to their beds, perhaps in a straightjacket, your nerves are in shreds and your mind in pieces at the moment. Seeing a mad person shouting or talking to themselves, means you are making an exhibition of yourself and possibly harming your interests or reputation as a result. A madman or madwoman laughing means it is best to put off new financial ventures for the time being, and one crying means you will receive an unexpected but welcome gift. Being mad yourself means you love someone else and that they love you; killing someone else who is mad indicates that a misdeed in the past will now catch up with you and bring unpleasant results.

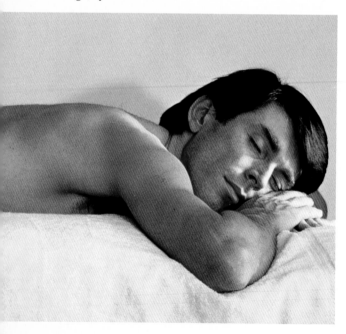

A handsome man is a sign of health and happiness

Man
An attractive male in a dream is a sign of happiness and health, and an ugly one denotes your uncertainty in emotional matters. If you dream of a tall man it means that you are setting your sights too high and you should adjust them, while a short man reveals that you have an adaptable, practical nature. Dreaming about a deaf man indicates that a secret to which you are privy must not be revealed to others, whatever happens; a blind man reflects the fact that you are restless and lack confidence.

Martyr
Being a martyr in a dream indicates that you have the characteristics of one yourself, being a generous and honest person who will make great sacrifices for something you believe in. Martyrdom in dreams also shows that in the future you will be decisive enough to bring all your personal projects to a successful conclusion. Seeing someone else dying for their beliefs is a sign that you should not start getting things out of proportion or exaggerating their importance.

Nun
Most dreams involving nuns reflect a rather proud and ambitious personality. They show that you are close to achieving a result from a project at work and so should not harm this in any way by being big-headed, as you are prone to be. A young nun is a symbol of desires not being fulfilled, and an old one of an experience which could be useful at some point in the future. Dreaming about a nun who is singing is a promise of ongoing happiness with the person you love most; if the nun is dead, on the other hand, a fairly serious illness will affect someone dear to you.

Old person
Dreaming of an old person who is poor means your apprehension about something is unjustified; a rich one indicates future delays and hindrances in your life; a sick one shows your adaptability to your surroundings; and a dead one means financial benefits are in prospect for you. Seeing an old person who is drunk means you are feeling uncertain and insecure, but if the old person is a hunchback, you will be fortunate and successful in matters of romance.

Orphan
The figure of an orphan in dreams generally reflects unhappiness and misfortunes. A child that has lost both its parents indicates that you have serious worries about the future, while if it has lost only its mother, there are family problems on the horizon. If it is without a father, you are gradually being overcome by sadness. If you dream about being an orphan yourself, it indicates promises not being kept. Welcoming an orphan into your home and looking after him or her means the conclusion of a particular project at work.

Painter
Dreaming about a painter exhibiting his work should be regarded as a warning: you are at a vital stage in your work,

and involved in important projects which will be fundamental to your future career. However, things will turn out well eventually.

Police

In a dream as in real life, the sight of a policeman is usually reassuring and should inspire confidence. Although you are going through a difficult time where work is concerned, dreaming of a policeman indicates that you will be helped by the person you love, and his or her affection will help you regain your self-confidence, which is waning fast at the moment. If you get into trouble with the police in a dream, there is no cause for alarm as the dream actually indicates lasting happiness and well-being. Being a policeman yourself in a dream shows that you have a (probably unconscious) desire to meddle in things which do not concern you.

Porter

Seeing a porter carrying someone's luggage in a dream shows that there is a certain amount of hostility going on behind your back, though if the porter is using a trolley, a piece of work you are involved in will turn out very much to your advantage. Being a porter yourself shows fatigue and exhaustion caused by overwork.

Priest

Dreaming of a priest in a church shows that others, some of whom you know about and some of whom you do not, are looking after your interests. A priest sitting in a confessional indicates that you are harbouring unfounded suspicions. If he is celebrating communion, you will be helped and counselled by people in authority. A priest giving a sermon means you will receive an indication of someone else's concern for you, and if he is blessing his congregation, you are being selfish, vain and materialistic.

Rabbi

Dreaming about a rabbi in his synagogue foretells good news from a very long way away; if he is preaching, it means you will make an advantageous agreement; and if he is reading, it indicates your present difficulties are being smoothed over. If he is discussing something with others, it shows that you are in an unnecessary state of gloom and despondency over some situation, but if you can pull yourself together and try not to spend too much time pondering, you will see how unimportant these temporary problems really are. Speaking to a rabbi means you are feeling pleased with the way life is going at the moment.

Rag-and-bone man

A rag-and-bone man buying something in a dream usually means a minor tiff between you and your partner, while if he is selling something, the outlook for an important project you are involved in at work is a bright one. If you are a rag-and-bone man in your dream, it means you are involved in a risky and hazardous venture which could prove to be expensive.

Smuggler

Being a smuggler yourself in a dream means you lack self-discipline and tend to get involved in short-lived, risky exploits that may land you in trouble. Seeing a smuggler at work, or being chased or arrested, indicates rash, hastily-made decisions.

A soldier on the battlefield suggests a generation gap

Soldier

Dreaming of a soldier within barracks marks the end of a worry which has been tormenting you for a long time. A soldier in the street shows that you are getting mental stimulation from work, and one on parade means someone has a greater interest in you than you may realize. A soldier on the battleground means a difficult time with somebody much younger than yourself, and if you are a soldier yourself in your dream, it suggests you feel very strongly about something but have trouble persuading others to share your view.

Speaker
Dreaming of an orator standing on a platform means disagreements and disputes with important people, while if he or she is in church, you are being critical of a friend, perhaps justifiably. A person making a political speech shows that you have to explain some aspect of your behaviour to the person you love. Making any kind of speech yourself means you have a grievance which you are keeping close to your chest.

Stranger
Any appearance by someone you do not recognize in your dream indicates long-lasting friendships and faithfulness in love.

Tramp
Dreaming of an old tramp is a sign of your depression and delusion. A male tramp indicates an unexpected meeting with someone, and a female one, surprising events of a romantic kind. If you are the tramp in your dream, you need to call on all your reserves of common sense and decisiveness to deal with some very difficult obstacles. If you have a partner, dreaming of being a tramp reveals that the few minor arguments you have in store will serve only to strengthen the relationship.

Vagabond
A vagabond in a dream is a symbol of your excessively lofty ambitions. If the vagabonds you dream of are drunk, it means someone is misunderstanding your motives, and if they are old, you are about to reach a new agreement. If your dream involves helping a vagabond or down-and-out, you have some important decisions to make. If you dream of being a vagabond yourself, it means you have a craving for more independence.

Virgin
A virgin is a symbol in dreams of happiness and joy, though a dead virgin means unexpected complications at work. If your dream involves starting a relationship with someone who is a virgin, you are about to begin a period where fortune smiles on you in everything you do. If you dream about being a virgin yourself, it suggests you are being naive at the moment and this is causing you to drop in other peoples' estimation.

Waiter or waitress
Dreaming of a waiter or waitress in a hotel is a sign of good luck, especially if it is a waitress. But if they serve you in your own or someone else's house, it indicates family problems

If a woman features in your dream negative qualities are indicated

and disagreements. A waiter or waitress dressed in spotless black and white livery is a sign that there is danger just around the corner.

Woman
Surprisingly enough, any woman in a dream – whether she is young or old, naked or richly dressed, beautiful or ugly – indicates insincerity, uncertainty, bitterness and resentment. A woman in the company of a man, however, is a symbol of confidence and decisiveness.

Family

Brother
Dreaming about an older brother denotes a courageous personality, while the appearance of a younger brother in a dream portends a family argument. A brother who behaves kindly towards you in the dream, actually suggests a break with a friend, but if the brother behaves badly in the dream, good luck is indicated.

Family
Dreaming about your own family suggests that there is important news on the horizon, while dreaming about any large family means that you are in a comfortable financial state but that you will have to make major sacrifices of some kind in the future. Dreaming about abandoning a family indicates financial problems.

Father or mother
Seeing your own father in a dream indicates that you should follow advice given to you by an older person; while embracing your father means that you ought to take up sensible suggestions which are being put to you by others. If your father appears healthy in the dream, you will shortly benefit from someone's support, but if he is ill, your faith in yourself is waning. If your father dies in the dream, it means you will come to occupy a responsible and respected position in which you will feel happy. To dream of a benevolent father shows that you are subject to passing enthusiasms, while to dream of a bad one shows that you are in good physical health.

It is very common to dream about your own mother. The dream indicates that you are having difficulties with your partner – although this state of things will not last for long if you take the hint and sort out the problem – and that you are turning back to your old family ties for emotional security. Seeing your mother crying means you are already anxious about something and there are more problems to come.

Godparent
Dreaming about someone else being a godparent signifies happiness and the recognition by someone of a kind deed that you did in the past. If you dream about being a godparent to a relative, you need to be astute and decisive if you are to take advantage of a favourable opportunity being offered to you. If you dream of being a godparent for a friend, you are going through a good period in your life.

Grandparent
If you dream about talking to your grandparents, it suggests that advice being given to you is both sound and useful. Dreaming about your grandparents on your father's side indicates sound business acumen, while those on your mother's side indicate gentleness combined with strong powers of persuasion. Dreaming that your grandparents have died is a sign that your business affairs – but not your health – are at risk.

Husband or wife
See *Love*

Mother-in-law
The appearance in a dream of a mother-in-law that you get on well with actually indicates arguments within your family. An elderly mother-in-law in a dream is a sign of your adaptability. If you argue with your mother-in-law in a dream, you will make an interesting new friend, while if you patch up your differences with her, there is pleasant news on the way.

Relative
Dreaming of a rich relative means you are feeling excessively vain about yourself, but dreaming of a poor one indicates unexpected financial benefits or income. Seeing a relative in a dream means you are not always faithful in your relationships with the opposite sex. Inviting a relative to your home means you are feeling decisive and self-confident; if they come for a meal, it means that you still have a lot to learn about getting on with other people, and should not be so argumentative.

Sister
Sisters represent the feminine principle in dreams. Dreaming of them suggests that your creativity, intuition, and emotions are being repressed. You must find suitable outlets for this side of your character, whether you are a man or a woman. Sisters also denote protection, and mean that whatever your worries – everything will turn out well eventually.

Son
To have a son in a dream (whether or not you actually have a son in real life) signifies success. An unmarried son reflects problems in your life, and a married one, worries connected with your family.

8
Places

Famous surrealist painters, such as Salvador Dali and Max Ernst, specialized in depicting the weirdly beautiful and uneasy landscapes we see in dreams. Powerful images of sinister deserts, strange rock formations, and unearthly seas continue to be potent fifty years later – for they are paintings inspired by the subconscious; such visual glimpses of it are often disturbing, but fascinating.

Psychologically, places in dreams are frequently said to represent the self and its structure: the outside of the building is the image you present to the world, its windows your eyes and how you use them, the basement the unconscious, the kitchen the practical heart of your personality and the bedroom your romantic and sexual self.

The rooms you see in your dream can therefore give useful clues about your state of mind, as can the actual condition of the house. If your dream home is clean, well-kept and pretty but contains a dark, dank cellar, you could be trying to hide something from yourself – something which is lurking in the depths of the unconscious.

Dreams of buildings are amongst the most common of all and always worth considering in this way, for surprising insights can result from careful thought. With their help, you may literally be able to put your house in order.

Institutional places, such as hospitals, schools and prisons, are said to symbolize our hidden attitudes towards authority and our parents. Travelling dreams involving roads are usually connected with our path through life itself, and may warn the dreamer of unexpected obstacles or be encouraging him or her to get a move on.

Places

Barn
Going into a barn or hay-loft in a dream indicates good luck and success with tasks you are currently involved in. If the barn falls down or catches fire there may be trouble in the air in your daily life.

Bazaar
Going into an eastern bazaar or buying things in one shows that you probably make decisions without proper reflection. But if the bazaar is full of toys or trinkets, it signifies that there is the chance of a pleasant encounter very soon.

Boat
If you dream about steering a boat through calm waters, your life will be calm and unruffled, but if the water is stormy, you can expect your life to be the same. A sinking boat suggests a hidden peril on the way.

Carnival
This is not a positive dream, as it suggests melancholy, suffering and disorder, while a masked carnival or ball indicates duplicity and dishonesty. Dreaming about taking part in a carnival procession points to an obstacle to be overcome.

Cemetery
Contrary to what one might expect, dreaming about a cemetery holds out great hope for the future: it indicates the fulfilment of many of your desires. Going to a cemetery with someone else is a sign of true friendship, while putting flowers on a grave denotes a sensitive, but also somewhat indecisive, personality.

Church
Seeing the outside of a church in a dream denotes good fortune, but going into one suggests you are being plagued with anxieties. Praying in a church is a sign of pleasure and comfort, while going into church dressed in mourning indicates a marriage in the near future.

City
Dreaming about a big city shows you have ambitious ideals, and if you find yourself living in a big city in the dream, these ideals will shortly be realized.

Convent
Seeing a convent in a dream is a sign of change and new developments. Dreaming about going into one or living in it suggests you have an openness, generosity and friendli-

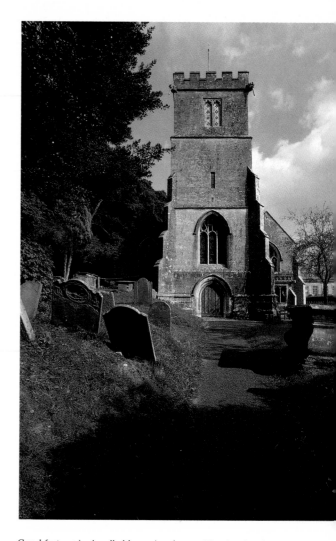

Good fortune is signalled by seeing the outside of a church

ness which makes you popular with others; and any dream involving a convent has generally favourable connotations for your welfare.

Corridor
Corridors appear frequently in dreams. If the corridor is a narrow one, there are possible losses of some kind in store for you, while a wide one reflects your considerable ambition. A dark corridor is a sign of worries looming on the horizon, and a brightly-lit one shows misunderstandings being cleared up.

Court

A magistrates' court in a dream indicates initiative and enterprise, while a cirminal court suggests that a decision of consequence needs to be taken very soon. A court martial shows that you are concerned about someone whose merits are unrecognized by others. Being a witness in court means you are about to overcome a difficult obstacle, but being taken to court yourself can often be a premonition of something unpleasant.

Courtyard

A dream in which a courtyard features is an optimistic one, indicating hopes being fulfilled, while if there are children or animals in the courtyard it suggests that you have managed to skirt dangers that were placed in your path.

Dormitory

A dormitory or ward in a hospital in a dream heralds visits from relatives, while a school or college dormitory indicates that you are subconsciously mulling over several plans for the future.

If you find your way through the jungle your path in life is clear

Farm

Seeing a prosperous, well-tended farm in a dream signifies good financial prospects: you will soon make a profit as a result of an astute business decision. If you own a farm yourself in the dream, you will be helped in your work by people who have more expertise than you, while if you are working on a farm, you will enjoy an advantage or benefit that your colleagues do not have. Selling a farm indicates that you are likely to have unpleasant disagreements with a new acquaintance. A farmhouse on fire in a dream reveals that you have enthusiasm and energy.

Frontier

Being on the border between two countries in a dream means that you are very good at adapting to different situations, but crossing over it means you have a sentimental side which is not doing you any good and you would be well-advised to cultivate more objectivity.

Garage

Dreaming of a garage with many new cars suggests that an older person will help you over an obstacle which you thought was insurmountable, while if the garage contains old cars that need repairing, you will gain a great deal by co-operating with someone else.

House

There are many different meanings to the symbol of a house in a dream, depending on what type of house it is and where it is. Building your own house reflects confidence in your own abilities and the likelihood of success in something you are doing, while moving house indicates worries relating to money. A house in the country indicates peace and tranquillity, and an empty house, a low income. A new house indicates a busy social life.

Jungle

Dreaming about a jungle full of dense trees, plants and creepers is a warning to the dreamer. If you get lost or stuck in the jungle, there are major problems lying in wait for you, but if you manage to make your way through the vegetation without too much trouble, you will also overcome difficulties in your real life.

Laboratory

This dream is a sign that you are in some kind of danger. This could involve your health (exhaustion, overwork), your state of mind (major depression), or your relationship with your partner, perhaps through a lack of mutual understanding and appreciation. However, these problems in store will probably only be temporary and will soon be resolved.

Library

A library in a dream is normally a favourable indication – whether it is a public or a private library – for it shows that the dreamer has a strong sense of responsibility, as well as self-confidence.

Lighthouse

A very bright lighthouse shining through the night in a dream indicates that you are free to choose from a number of exciting opportunities ahead of you. If it shines constantly, it signifies strength of will, but if it goes on and off, it shows that you have repressed feelings about somebody to resolve.

It bodes well for relationships if you dream about a market

Market

Dreaming about a market is a favourable omen in a dream, particularly if you are unattached. This dream shows you have a high degree of flexibility which will stand you in good stead in your work, as well as an open-minded personality which allows you to form long-lasting relationships with people. If you are not in love with anyone at the moment this dream indicates that you soon will be falling in love. You can also expect some other pleasant surprise which will make you particularly happy. If you are a married woman on the other hand, a market signifies imminent jealousy and betrayal.

Mill

Seeing either a windmill with its sails turning, or a watermill with its wheel revolving, in a dream means that an important project you were involved in at work will be a success and will bring you both job satisfaction and respect. If the mill is derelict or simply not working, both your work and your relationship with your partner are stagnating at the moment, and if you do not make an effort to change matters the situation could get worse.

Museum

If you dream about going to a museum, it is likely that you are going through a period of unhappiness and boredom. You ought to try to find new interests and get involved in new activities or the situation will go from bad to worse. If you visit a museum of ancient civilisations in the dream, the main cause of your unhappiness at the moment is that you feel disappointed because someone does not love you as much as you thought; if the museum contains sculptures or statues of any kind, your depression is caused simply by the fact that you are working too hard. A museum of the prehistoric era, perhaps containing dinosaurs, indicates that you will meet new acquaintances who will turn out to be very important in the future.

Overseas

Dreaming about any foreign country means you are somewhat childish and unreliable and unless you can get rid of these traits you will lose the respect and trust of those dear to you. Making a short visit overseas indicates insincerity on the part of yourself or someone else, and if you dream about emigrating, it is an indication that you wish to escape the interference of those around you.

Palace
See *Fantasy*

Pier

If you dream about being on a pier and looking out to sea, you are a rather nervous, restless person, engaged in a constant and unsuccessful search for personal fulfilment. Fortunately, someone is about to come into your life who will change this unhappy state of affairs. If you dream about fishing from a pier, you will soon receive some very happy news. If there are amusements on the pier, you are playing with someone else's affections and doing all of the taking in a relationship but none of the giving.

Police station

Being summoned yourself to a police station in a dream to give a statement suggests that you should try to get over your anger towards a friend you feel has let you down. Going into a police station shows your involvement in a difficult venture; coming out of one indicates that you will form a new friendship with someone of the opposite sex which could be misinterpreted by your partner.

Pub or inn

If you see any kind of pub or bar in your dreams, you have feelings for someone who does not return them. Going into a pub in a dream means someone you trust may be deceiving you. If you go in with someone else it suggests you are wasting precious time on a worthless project. Eating in a pub means a woman will lie to you, and drinking in one means you will receive praise shortly which may not be entirely heartfelt. A pub with drunks in it indicates possible enmity arising from your current social and professional position.

Dreaming about staying in an inn means that there may be a major business failure on the way with a consequent loss of money. Where lovers are concerned, this dream can mean their partner will go off with someone else.

Quarry
The meaning of this dream depends on what is being quarried. A chalk quarry presages financial problems, while coal being quarried indicates your high level of energy, and stone, the possibility of a journey.

Restaurant
See *Food*

Road
This is a symbol which can have several different meanings. A road sloping downhill indicates your differences of opinion with relatives, and an uphill one denotes the painful problems which you have to face in real life. A wide road means your relationships are untroubled at present and a narrow one foretells a strange meeting or encounter. Walking along a road in your dream means that your honest intentions will receive their own reward.

Room
A waiting room in a dream reflects your uncertainty about a work project which looks promising but which could go wrong. A ballroom indicates that emotional problems are looming, and a games room shows that suggestions being put forward may not be all that they seem. A dining room signifies your annoyingly obstinate behaviour, and a living room foretells unexpected guests.

School
A primary school in a dream means there are aspects of your behaviour that need to be changed; a secondary school, that you have a choice to make from a great number of options. A boarding school represents the support you are getting from friends at the moment, and a private school means you need to take precautions against potential risks. If you dream about going back to school, you will see some of your financial ventures finally being successful. If you are given a school report, it means you need to take a look at the reasons for your partner's unpredictable behaviour, and if you are given someone else's, you will suffer a loss of money.

Stable
If the stable has one or more donkeys in it, there are business problems ahead, but if it contains horses, prosperity and well-being are likely. If you dream about going to sleep in a stable, your business affairs are guaranteed to be a success. Dreaming of a cowshed with cows in it foretells a major achievement or success, while a sheepfold indicates your over-sensitivity.

Stage
Dreaming of a stage in a theatre symbolizes embitterment caused by something involving the opposite sex. If the stage projects out into the audience, it reflects a missed opportunity. If it has scenery on it, it shows you are involved in a long and hard search for anything which gives

Prosperity awaits you if you dream of horses in a stable

pleasure. A stage with actors performing on it means you are about to make an interesting discovery, and if you are on it yourself, making a speech or acting, you are showing totally unjustified jealousy which can only lead to the end of a relationship.

Station

A railway station in a dream heralds important news connected with work. If you are arriving at a station or departing from it in your dream, you are waiting patiently for the results of a major project you are involved in, but if you are meeting someone else at the station, the dream shows you will be helped in your career by someone who wields a great deal of influence. If the train you are waiting for is late, it means you should not move too quickly in a new relationship, but you ought to allow it time to develop as naturally as possible.

A stage with scenery means you are having a hard time

Swimming pool

Dreaming about a swimming pool full of water means prospects at work have never been better, and you should seize on any opportunities given to you, because they will not be there for very long. If the pool is empty, you are being unfair in your assessment of someone you have just met. If it is a very large pool, you have thought out a new project at work in considerable detail and you are hoping it will further increase your standing among the people you work with. Swimming in a pool yourself means this would be a good time to finish something you have left.

Theatre

Dreaming of a large theatre means you are entertaining desires which can never be realized, and a small one indicates practicality and helpfulness. A brightly-lit theatre indicates that you will confront situations in which appearances will be deceiving. If you go to see a play in your dream, you will receive news – which could be either good

or bad – from a long way away. Dreaming of an operating theatre is a sign of a weak personality.

Tower

A bell tower in a dream indicates particularly good relations with people at work, while a tower being knocked down indicates both fatigue and obstinacy. A leaning tower shows you have considerable inner resources. If the tower is very high, you will be involved in a potentially compromising situation.

Watch out for a compromising situation if you dream of a tower

A village in the distance warns you to look before you leap

Travelling

Travelling for pleasure in your dreams is a sign that you are taking a well-deserved rest, and travelling on business suggests you will find a favourable solution to a problem. If your journey is a short one, it reflects the fact that you are nervy and irritable, and if it is a long one, you can expect to make a new and interesting friend.

University

Applying to get into university in your dream means you are of a very inventive turn of mind and very strong-willed, but actually going to a university in a dream suggests you are moody and given to alternating elation and depression. If your dream involves being a lecturer or professor, it means you are going through a period of happiness in every aspect of your life. Graduating from university in a dream indicates a fresh challenge in your work environment, possibly involving a promotion or increase in responsibility, or even a new job.

Verandah or balcony

Dreaming of a verandah with flowers on it indicates that a pleasant surprise is in store, and one with green plants on it means renewed hope and ambition for a project you are involved in at work. If you dream about reading a book while sitting on a verandah or balcony, you will eventually reach a situation of complete harmony with your partner, even if things have been rather unpredictable up until now.

Villa

Dreaming of a magnificent villa with a beautiful garden means that your illusions will be destroyed and you will have to set your sights lower.

Village

Seeing a village in the distance in a dream is a warning that what may seem like a golden opportunity could have damaging consequences. If you dream that you live in a village, or find yourself in one, it means you are contented.

9
Food, Diet and Health

'Many's the long night I've dreamed of cheese — toasted, mostly', says Ben Gunn, the marooned and hungry pirate in *Treasure Island*. Strict dieters have confessed to similar longings as their dreaming minds create the large, delicious and fattening meals they are trying to avoid. So before looking at the considerable symbolism of food, always consult your stomach. A food dream could be simple wish-fulfilment.

Food is also a very emotional subject, stirring buried memories of babyhood when nourishment and loving attention were closely connected for both mother and child. Phrases such as 'starved of affection' and 'hungry for love' reveal just how deep these links go.

By now you will have realized the mind's ability to turn language into visual images and jokes. So if you are eaten up with emotion or thirst for knowledge you can expect your dreams to come up with appropriate pictures to match – which is food for thought.

Other foods are ancient symbols. Bread, for instance, is closely linked with Christian teachings representing the body of Christ in Holy Communion. It is known as the 'staff of life' and is also a slang term for money. Fruit symbolizes harvest and things coming to fruition.

Health dreams – unless you are a hypochondriac – are generally favourable and easy to understand. Perhaps you are sick of some problem in your life and longing for circumstances to improve? Your subconscious may be working hard to tell you that everything will be better soon. Doctors and nurses are usually kind, caring figures in dreams – and again are there to help you. Frightening childhood hospital experiences may also recur in dreams – their message is also positive. You are still alive, and therefore your fears are no longer appropriate; your mind is showing you the experience so that you can be free from remembered terrors.

Food and Diet

Banquet

This is one of the many symbols which means the opposite of what one might expect. Being present at a banquet indicates problems such as illness, a feud, having a rival in love, or depression.

Biting

See *Sensations*

Bread

A loaf of brown bread in a dream is a sign of major financial gains, while a white one signifies that you are forming projects for the future. A warm loaf reflects your partner putting your courage and faithfulness to the test. A stale loaf means you are about to enter a short period of discouragement and unhappiness, and an overcooked or burnt one means you should not make a fool of yourself by getting involved in something pointless and time-wasting. Buying a loaf of bread means excellent prospects on the work front, and eating one means you need to be more aware of your own responsibilities.

Breakfast

Starting a new day with a large, healthy meal is a good habit: in a dream it suggests promise for future projects and tasks, and success for any initiatives you may take.

If you dream of chocolate with nuts, ask yourself if you are bored

Chocolate

Dreaming about chocolate reflects your current state of well-being and ease, while eating it means there may be an unexpected loss of money or a major item of expense. Chocolate with nuts in it suggests boredom, while filled chocolate of any kind symbolizes fleeting pleasures.

Cream buns and tarts

Dreaming of a cream bun or tart signifies the arrival of a pleasant piece of news, while a chocolate tart shows present illness or fatigue. An apple pie or tart means you can expect a reward, and a cherry tart indicates you will make limited financial gains. A piping hot tart means that you will have an unforgettable experience together with your partner.

Diet

Being on a diet after an illness symbolizes pointless anxieties and a feeling of resignation. Dieting to get thinner, on the other hand, indicates good fortune in business, and being on a vegetarian diet in a dream suggests that you have trustworthy friends.

Dining

The precise meaning of having dinner in a dream depends on the circumstances. Dining at home means you will soon be involved in new projects and initiatives. Being invited to dinner at someone else's house may indicate a journey. Having dinner on a train or aeroplane suggests deep-seated desires and longings that are not being fulfilled.

Drinking

Having a drink from a crystal-clear fountain in a dream indicates future health and happiness. Giving a drink to someone who is thirsty shows that you are by nature a generous and kind-hearted person. Drinking milk or wine signifies health and happiness, but drinking dirty or muddy water means you are getting involved in matters which are not really your concern. Drinking a toast can have various meanings depending on why the toast is being drunk – a wedding, a birthday, a business function – but in general it signifies the arrival of either an unexpected but very welcome guest or piece of news.

A drink of cold tea in a dream indicates that there will be a gap or break in an emotional relationship of yours, while hot tea shows intelligence and sharp-wittedness. Tea with milk in it reflects your good sense and reason; and lemon tea, reserved, cautious behaviour. Generally speaking, if your dream involves drinking tea, you will manage to break free from the influence of others at work.

Eating

Most dreams involving eating symbolize physical and spiritual health, though the precise meaning depends on what is being eaten and how it is being eaten. Eating standing up suggests that you are doing things too hurriedly and not giving them enough thought. Eating with combine a vivid imagination with a decisive personality; however, if someone else forces you to fast, it reflects uncertainty in your life. If you stop eating because of illness in the dream, this shows that you have a low level of physical or mental stamina, while if you dream of being too poor to buy food, this signifies that in real life you will experience a change for the better.

Fatness
Dreaming about being fat indicates poor health, physical weakness, and anxiety. If you are in love it can also mean that there will be deceitfulness and a possible breakdown in relations with your partner.

Food
Dreaming about food can have different implications depending on precisely what the food is. If there are large quantities involved, or you eat too much, this shows that you hold ambiguous or unclear intentions in regard to a person or project, while if there is not enough to eat, a period of tranquillity and prosperity is on the way.

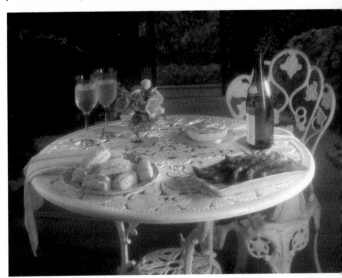

Anticipate prosperity if an elegant sufficiency of food appears.

Fruit
The meaning of this dream depends on the type of fruit involved, but in most cases it is a favourable sign. Fruit symbolizes harvest and things coming to fruition, while the apple is traditionally the fruit of the knowledge of good and evil that tempted Eve in the Garden of Eden. Dreaming about a bowl of fruit shows that you are, or soon will be, enjoying excellent health and prosperity and a happy domestic life. Bitter or rotten fruit, on the other hand, is a sign of discord or sadness.

Eating in a dream is usually a sign of well-being

your hands indicates that you feel very angry and disillusioned with your partner. Eating in secret indicates both nostalgia for the past and also ill-humour.

Eggs
Easter eggs in a dream symbolize an important statement or report being made at work. Fresh eggs mean opportunities are being presented to you on a plate, but rotten eggs indicate that things will be going against you. If you buy eggs in your dream, you will be able to make good use of the extra financial resources which are coming your way.

Famine
A famine in a dream actually indicates prosperity, well-being, strong friendship and lasting love.

Fasting
If you voluntarily go without food for a long time in your dream – perhaps as an act of penitence – it means you

A pizza piled high with toppings is a good sign for relationships

Hunger
This is the classic example of a dream signifying its opposite: if you, or other people, are hungry, it means both good luck and a healthy financial situation. In fact, strange as it may seem, the more intense the hunger, the more fortune is likely to smile on you.

Meat
Any dream which involves buying meat or cooking it is a sign of your prosperity, but eating meat reflects your disagreements with someone. Frozen or packaged meat is a symbol of falsehood and deception, and rotting meat means your health may be at risk in some way.

Pizza
Dreaming of a pizza piled high with toppings indicates a strengthening of relationships, but dreaming of just an ordinary pizza, with the customary amount of cheese and tomato, shows your lack of concentration and consistency at work. A burned pizza indicates an unexpected success in relations with the opposite sex. If you dream about making a pizza, you are entering a period which is favourable from every point of view, and if you buy one, you will easily get round any obstacles which are being placed in your path at work. Eating a pizza shows that you are throwing yourself wholeheartedly into a new activity.

Recipe
Reading or using a recipe in a dream shows that past financial setbacks have turned out to be less serious than you had thought. Writing a recipe down indicates that you have misjudged a person who has in reality a great deal of respect for you. Giving a recipe to someone else means you are very good at making the correct decision in any difficult situation that may arise.

Refreshments
Making refreshments, such as sandwiches or drinks, in a dream means you are steadily climbing up the career ladder which will eventually allow you to reach the lifestyle you were aiming for. Buying them means your feelings toward your partner, and theirs toward you, are serious and sincere. Taking any kind of refreshment means you are likely to enjoy perfect health.

Restaurant
Dreaming of a restaurant in a town symbolizes the fact that someone you know is keeping a secret, while one in the country means that problems are on the way for you. A crowded restaurant indicates difficulties with your partner caused by your timidity, and an empty one, a worrying emotional problem caused by your partner's unpredictable behaviour. If you have a meal in a restaurant in a dream, it shows that you will receive an attractive proposition, perhaps connected with your work.

Supper
Cooking supper in a dream suggests that a short period of belt-tightening is in order because of your financial situation. If the meal is for more than one person it indicates your mood of calm and serenity, but if it is for one it reflects presumptuous, arrogant behaviour.

Tighten your belt if you find yourself cooking supper in a dream

Health

Affliction
Any affliction, or illness, in a dream heralds a change in your domestic situation such as moving house. As far as love is concerned, being afflicted or ill in a dream means you need to take great care in choosing the partner who is right for you.

Convalescence
Dreaming that you are taking time off while recovering from a major illness has favourable implications entirely unconnected with your health: it signifies a major success is imminent in your work.

Diagnosis
A diagnosis is an auspicious sign. Diagnosing an illness actually means your love for someone is growing, while a favourable diagnosis – the doctor telling you there is nothing wrong – indicates security in your job.

Doctor
A doctor who appears in a dream indicates good health and fortune.

Fever
A dream involving a fever in fact indicates the end of a period of ill health and the beginning of renewed energy and vitality. If you are ill when you dream about a fever, you will get well very soon.

Going mad
Going mad in a dream signifies that the very opposite is true in real life: it indicates that you are very intelligent, have a secure business and are in good health. Going mad through love in a dream means there are interesting changes in the offing.

Health
A healthy man in a dream foreshadows a brilliant career full of satisfactions, but a healthy woman suggests bitterness and resentment for a misdeed in the past. Eating a healthy meal in a dream means that your feelings towards your partner now are not the same as they used to be.

Hospital
An ordinary hospital in a dream indicates a depressed, melancholic person, while a field hospital in a war means you are missing someone who is a long way away, and any other kind of military hospital reflects a worrying piece of news. A psychiatric hospital indicates stormy family relationships. If you see any kind of hospital, you are

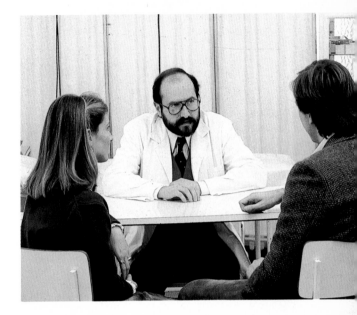
Good health and luck are yours if a doctor features in your dream

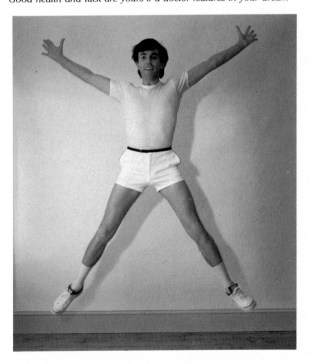
You'll follow a brilliant career if you dream of a healthy man

probably being stricken by worries which you need to overcome, and if you go inside one for any reason, whether as a patient or visitor, your health is on the mend and you are being exceptionally decisive. Coming out of a hospital indicates a solution is being found to a long-standing and tricky problem.

Illness
Dreaming about being bedridden through any type of illness indicates that you could succumb to a temptation which may harm you in the longer term. If someone else is sick, it suggests you should keep a close eye on any potential rivals, either at work or in love, who are threatening to make life difficult for you.

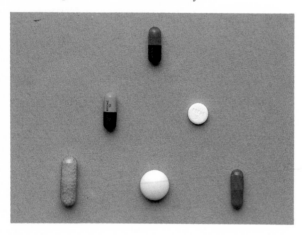

Daring and freedom from dependency are indicated by loose pills

Leprosy
If you dream about having leprosy yourself, it suggests that you are already worried about a situation and that further problems might crop up to complicate things even more. It can also mean that you feel guilty about your behaviour towards someone. Dreaming of others with leprosy suggests you have enemies.

Medicine
If you dream about taking a medicine which leaves a bitter taste in your mouth, this is an optimistic omen. You will come to realize that a predicament or person which you thought was a hindrance can actually be of great help to you. Although there will also be problems in your relationship with your partner, these will only serve to strengthen the ties between you.

Mental hospital
This is a fairly common subject to dream about: it is neither the bringer of good or bad tidings, but simply a warning. If you are in a psychiatric hospital of some kind in the dream,

there is something causing you bewilderment or incomprehension in your life, and you need to do something about it pretty quickly or it will cause you problems. If you dream about visiting one, it suggests differences between you and your superiors or your parents. Leaving one is a symbol of regret for something that has happened but there is no need to be afraid as better times are coming.

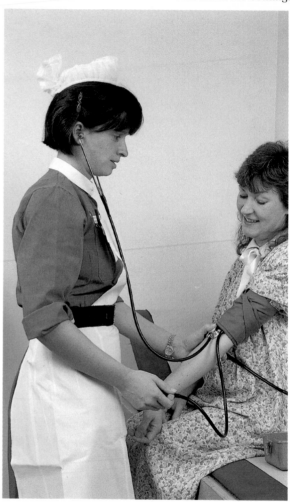

You feel unwanted if a nurse is looking after you in a dream

Nurse
Seeing a nurse at work in a dream indicates that prosperity and important financial gains are on the way; a nurse looking after children indicates a faithful relationship with your partner. However, being looked after by a nurse means you feel unwanted at the moment. Pretending to be a nurse yourself means you will receive some news which is potentially very advantageous.

Operation

Being operated on in hospital in a dream means you like to have the attention of others focused on you all the time, but operating on someone else yourself means you are a generous and caring type of person. Performing a heart transplant means you will succeed in all your plans, and brain surgery means you have still to overcome a major obstacle. Watching almost any kind of operation indicates weakness of character.

Pain

See *Sensations*

Pharmacy

A pharmacy is a warning signal when it appears in a dream: going into one means you should pay more attention to your choice of friends. If you go in during the day in your dream, a slight illness or injury is in prospect, but if you go into an all-night chemist's, there may be a more serious illness involved.

Pills

Loose pills in dreams indicate that you will undertake a daring venture with many risks involved which will help you get away from your psychological dependence on someone or something. Pills in a bottle reflect your indecision and timidity: if only you could have a little more confidence in your abilities, the sky would be the limit. If the pills are laxatives, you will shortly reach a more equable relationship with your partner; if they are headache pills, you will experience a disappointment connected with your work.

Sore

A sore in a dream can be just as unpleasant as it is in real life. It means you are entering a critical period as far as your future career is concerned; unless you think carefully before making any decision, you could stand to lose out financially. If you have a sore on your hand, you will manage to sort out problems facing you at work easily, and if it is on your arm, you will be able to benefit from close co-operation between you and another person at work. A sore on your face in a dream promises success for a venture you have put money into.

Wound

Being wounded, or wounding someone else, means the opposite of what one might expect in dreams: if you are young, it is a symbol of love, and if you are in business, it represents profits and prosperity.

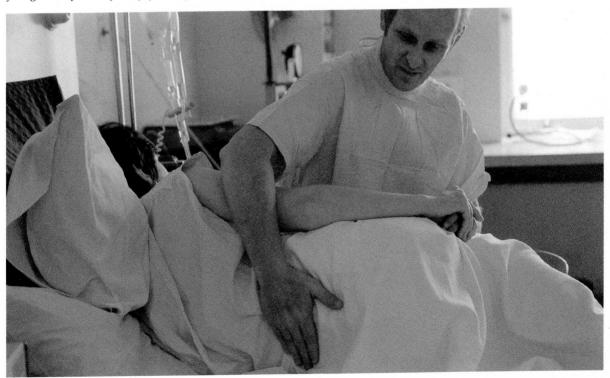

If you dream of being operated on in hospital, you are a bit of an attention-seeker

10
Animals

In Ancient Greece and Rome, seers believed that signs and portents of the future often appeared in the shape of animals and birds. Some of their ideas have come down through the centuries, surviving in old superstitions such as wishing on a white horse, thinking it lucky if a black cat crosses your path, and so on. These ideas, even if you do not consciously recall them, can influence your dreams.

Other creatures have been given personalities which seem to fit, in phrases like 'busy as a bee', or 'strong as an ox' or 'cunning like a fox'. Many of these animals in the form of stuffed toys had special places in our hearts when we were children. They were loyal friends and comforters, or perhaps favourite characters in a much-loved bedtime story or television programme. Creatures harking back to childhood are extremely personal and do not mean the same for everyone – so you must first consult your own memories before applying any broader, traditional meanings.

Astrology provides another source of animal symbolism which your subconscious could easily have picked up. Fish, lions, bulls and rams represent signs of the zodiac. Countries also have national animals – the American Eagle, British Lion and Russian Bear, for instance.

Psychologically, animals are said to represent parts of our personality or our 'animal' nature – the sensual, sexual side of every human being. Freud's theories on the interpretation of dreams were primarily sexual. He believed that the mind translated subconscious fears and wishes into dream images – creating clever disguises through a metaphorical language. Animal images can be some of the most rewarding, if difficult, to analyse in dreams – so consult the meanings given in this chapter, and see if you can add a few of your own.

Animals

Alligator or crocodile
An alligator or crocodile in a dream is a warning that you need to watch out for a powerful enemy who may be creeping up on you behind your back.

Bear
Dreaming about a bear is a reminder of major problems and the possible presence of an adversary or rival in your life. But killing a bear is a symbol of overcoming one's difficulties and defeating the adversary.

Beetle
Seeing a flying beetle in a dream is an indication of good fortune in everything you do (love, work, finances) and with everyone you meet, from shop assistants to lovers. A beetle beating against some kind of obstacle and falling to the ground is a sign that projects you are involved in will not be completed until much later than expected.

Cat
The well-known black cat crossing one's path also brings good luck if seen in a dream. Generally speaking, though, cats are not a good omen, suggesting unfaithfulness in love and complications in one's working life. Killing a cat means you are causing your enemies discomfort.

Although a kitten is normally a good omen in dreams, this is not the case if it bites or scratches anyone: it shows that your partner is deceiving you in some way.

Crow
The crow, with its black body and wings, is not a good omen: it is a harbinger of disappointment, financial worries and health problems. Hearing its cawing in your sleep is a symbol of unpleasant occurrences to come.

Dog
Most dreams involving dogs mean that we can expect agreeable events to occur as the result of a friend's actions. But a growling dog in a dream indicates that a friend cannot necessarily be trusted, and a dog that bites someone means you are making things difficult for yourself by being obstinate. A barking dog signifies imminent danger and a howling dog also warns of impending misfortune or calamity.

Dove
Dreaming of a turtle dove in its nest is a sign of unexpected gains and emotional happiness, especially if it is cooing. A wounded turtle dove means there are problems to be sorted out in your life; if it is dead, these problems may be major ones.

Eagle
If you dream of this beautiful bird soaring through the air it shows that you have high expectations of yourself and will one day see your ambitions realized. If the eagle is wounded or dead, however, your reputation will suffer.

You must have been bold recently if you dream of a flight of gulls

You may be wasting your time on a project if you ride in a hunt

Eel
Dreaming about an eel indicates either finding work, or changing jobs, at sometime in the very near future, but the job may be difficult and your new boss may be hard to get on with. A dead eel symbolizes getting the upper hand over someone who is trying to create problems for you.

Elephant
A dream about an elephant is a favourable indication, suggesting strength, health, and also a possible association in the future with somebody important.

Flight of birds
A flight of swallows in a dream is an omen of unexpected, and not necessarily pleasant news; a flight of gulls indicates recent bold, daring behaviour. A flight of ducks symbolizes an unbelievable stroke of good fortune, and any other large group of birds is likely to bring pleasant news of some kind.

Fox
The fox is a wily, sly and fast-moving creature, and in dreams signifies someone you dislike, possibly a passing acquaintance, or a rival in love. So if you dream about a fox, you need to take a close look at the potentially harmful activities of those around you.

Horse
A dream involving a horse is always a good sign, unless the horse is black all over, in which case mourning or grief is indicated. Riding a horse is a sign both of independence and happiness, though if the horse manages to unseat you, plans you have made are likely to go wrong. Finding a horseshoe in a dream is an extremely good omen.

Hounds
Following the hounds in a hunt in a dream means that research or similar work you are involved in is unlikely to be productive; while if you are attached, your partner may not trust you totally and you should look for ways to reassure him or her in this regard.

Jackal
See *Nightmares*

Lion
A lion is generally an animal which brings good luck, and if you dream about one it indicates a personal success or gain, although not necessarily a financial one. If the lion is roaring because it is enraged, you are anxious about the jealousy of someone close to you. Fighting with a lion means a fight or argument in real life.

Dreaming about a lioness is also a hopeful sign in dreams, especially if she is lying down with her cubs, in which case your family relationships will be happy ones.

Lizard
This is an unfavourable dream, indicating enemies lying in wait for you.

Look out for enemies if a lizard whizzes through your dream

Magpie
These elegant black and white birds with their thieving nature are not an auspicious omen in dreams: they

foreshadow problems within your family, which are likely to increase in seriousness in proportion to the number of magpies you see in your dreams.

Monkey
The monkey is an inauspicious sign, indicating that you are surrounded by lies and deceit.

Nightingale
This is a very happy omen to appear in a dream; it foretells joy, success and riches. If lovers dream about a nightingale, theirs will be a happy marriage. If you dream about a nightingale when you are ill, you will soon be on the mend. If you dream that you hear the song of the nightingale, you can expect fortune to smile on you in business matters and an advancement in your career.

Octopus
Any dream with an octopus in it signifies your spirit of adventure, while an octopus being killed or caught reflects your strong sense of moral right and wrong. An octopus attacking anyone in a dream means trouble in store.

Peacock
This magnificent bird has long been a symbol of pride and vanity, though in dreams it can also show that you are particularly aware and appreciative of someone else's beauty at the moment.

Pheasant
A pheasant is a favourable sign in dreams, and coming back from the hunt with a brace of pheasants shows great honours in prospect.

Pig
A pig in a dream can symbolize both good and bad luck. It suggests that something you are involved in will go wrong, but another venture – which you did not hold very high hopes of – will be a surprising success. Be careful with members of your family, as they may cause you some distress. If you dream about a pig just before you go off on a journey, it might be better to postpone it for a while.

If you dream about a sow coming towards you, there is good fortune on the way; but if it is walking or running away, then the future holds out little luck for you.

It is good luck to dream about a hare

Rabbit or hare

Dreaming of a rabbit usually brings good luck, and in many countries its foot, whether in real life or in dreams, is regarded as a particular symbol of good fortune. A rabbit in a dream also symbolizes prosperity and fertility. Sometimes it foretokens a move to a big city, or anywhere else which is crowded. A married woman dreaming about a rabbit can expect a new child. A rabbit crossing a road, on the other hand, denotes imminent danger.

Dreaming about a hare is a sign of good luck: if it is running towards you, close friends will soon be coming to see you, and a girl who dreams about a hare is likely to be on the verge of meeting her husband-to-be. A hare being coursed, however, means serious risks being faced.

A swimming swan is a sign of prosperity

Rat

Dreaming about these animals means that a large number of relatively small problems are on the way. For someone in love who dreams of rats there is an additional, but much greater, problem: you have an implacable rival who will stop at nothing to win your partner. If you are married, you can expect minor upsets caused by people who are supposed to be your friends.

Snake

See *Nightmares*

Stork

Despite its connotations, dreaming about a stork is not a good sign: it foretells a change, possibly a move, which will leave you worse off than before. If the stork is flying, there is the risk of your committing a crime, and if it is sitting in its nest, you are likely to have family problems.

Swan

Seeing a swan in a dream shows that pleasant news is on the way, while a swan swimming on a lake or pond indicates future prosperity and material well-being. Feed-ing a swan signifies happiness in love. A black swan, however, indicates that the future will be less pleasant.

Tiger

A sleeping tiger, or one in a cage, is harmless, and hence dreaming of one in this state is a sign of social advancement; but a tiger attacking a person or animal in a dream means there is serious danger on the horizon.

Unicorn

A unicorn is not a favourable sign in a dream: it suggests that you are facing problems which are being caused by people who are less pleasant and trustworthy than they seem on first acquaintance.

Vulture

See *Nightmares*

Wolf

See *Nightmares*

Zebra

A zebra in a dream is a warning sign: you should be very careful and keep your eyes open, otherwise something unpleasant could happen to you.

Keep your eyes skinned if a zebra comes into your dream

Acknowledgments

The Publishers thank the following for providing the photographs in this book:
Bridgeman Art Library/Musee de l'Orangerie Paris, Lauros – Giraudon 12; /King Street Galleries London 28; Tony Stone Associates/Ron Sutherland 14/M. Manheim 15 left.

The following photographs were taken specially for the Octopus Publishing Group Picture Library:
Martin Brigdale 49 left; Mike Busselle 48, 80 right, 88 left, 122; Ian Dawson 19, 31; Entwhistle/Canterbury Cathedral 45 left; John Freeman 43, 46, 51; Ray Gardner 58; Greg Germany 56; Andre Goulancourt (St Thomas Hospital Doulton tiles) 6, 44; Chris Harvey 70, 87 below; Michael Holford/Tate Gallery 40 left; James Jackson 82; Peter Johnson 42, 95 right; Chris Knaggs 40 right; Bob Langrish 93 above; Peter Loughran 49 right, 92, 93 below, 95 left; Sandra Lousada 17, 18 above, 23 left, 25, 34, 35, 62, 65, 79, 85 above, 86 below, 88 right, 89; Steve Lyne 26, 27; Duncan McNicol 38; Erwin Meyer/Vienna Kunsthistorisches Museum 66; John Miller 53; Colin Molyneux 54, 76; James Murphy 85 below; National Gallery, London 69; Mike O'Neill 24 left; Mike St. Maur Sheil 59 left; John Sims 52, 55, 59 right; Charlie Stebbings 33, 86 above; Ron Sutherland 24 right, 63 left and right; Norman Tozer 80 left; John Webb/ V. & A. 50 left,/Tate Gallery 74; Paul Williams 84